Sermon on the Mount
The Jesus Manifesto

A Commentary on Matthew 5 - 7 for Personal Devotional Use, Small Groups or Sunday School Classes, and Sermon Preparation for Pastors and Teachers

JesusWalk® Bible Study Series

by Dr. Ralph F. Wilson
Director, Joyful Heart Renewal Ministries

Additional books and reprint licenses are available at:
http://www.jesuswalk.com/books/manifesto.htm

Free Participant Guide handout sheets are available at:
http://www.jesuswalk.com/manifesto/manifesto-lesson-handouts.pdf

JesusWalk® Publications
Loomis, California

Paperback
ISBN-13: 978-0-9847340-0-9
ISBN-10: 0984734007

Library of Congress Control Number: 2011918832

Library of Congress subject headings:
Sermon on the mount
Bible. N.T. Matthew

Suggested Classifications
Library of Congress: BT380.2
Dewey Decimal System: 226.9

Published by JesusWalk® Publications, P.O. Box 565, Loomis, CA 95650-0565, USA.

JesusWalk is a registered trademark and Joyful Heart is a trademark of Joyful Heart Renewal Ministries.

Unless otherwise noted, all the Bible verses quoted are from the New International Version (International Bible Society, 1973, 1978), used by permission.

111017

Preface

Organized religion has tended to domesticate Jesus' teaching. In his day, part of Jesus' attraction was that he was untamed, unrestricted by the religious structures of his day. When he taught, he spoke with a clear authority that troubled and angered the religious elite. But the common people flocked to him. His words challenged their souls and their way of life, but they also brought hope and an

Gustave Doré, detail of "Jesus Preaching on the Mount" (*Jesus Prechant Sur La Montagne*, c. 1865), oil on canvas, 130 x 196 cm, private collection.

abiding peace to their lives. Jesus was setting aright a tragic misunderstanding and misinterpretation of God's true intention. When people were – and are – willing to repent from their wrong understandings and their un-Godly ways, they can enter a renewed Kingdom of God now and forever.

Our record of Jesus' life, ministry, and teaching covers the first four books of the New Testament – Matthew, Mark, Luke, and John – in all 89 chapters. This teaching seems to be distilled, however, in the three chapters that comprise Jesus' Sermon on the Mount (Matthew 5-7), probably his most definitive statement of how the Kingdom of God differed from what passed for religion in his day. I see it as the Jesus Manifesto.

Manifesto: "a written statement declaring publicly the intentions, motives, or views of its issuer."

His words were as radical in the first century as they are in the twenty-first. They possess a kind of raw force that cut us to the core of our lives. Many declare Jesus' words as a mere ideal, a hope, a pipe dream. But I believe that if we can understand what Jesus truly taught, absorb it into our spirit, and faithfully order our lives so that we can live it out here on earth, we can grow into the kind of Christians that he intends for us to be – real Christians, Jesus Christians, world-altering Christians of whom he will be proud.

Many in our day identify themselves as "born again" Christians, that is, believers who have begun a new life through the regenerating power of the Holy Spirit (John 3:1-8). This is essential. But if born again Christians don't grow into faithful, authentic disciples of Jesus, who know his ways and live them out with integrity, they bring discredit upon both Jesus and the truth of the new birth.

The Sermon on the Mount provides an ethical and philosophical framework within which we can order our lives as followers of Jesus who look and act like his disciples did in the first century. I commend this Sermon to you as an elixir for your souls.

This book is intended to help you grapple with and comprehend Jesus' teaching in the first century Jewish milieu in which it was first given. It is designed first to help individual believers deeply study his words. Then it is intended to provide Bible study leaders and teachers material for their groups and classes, and pastors as grist for pulpit preaching.

If you are already a Christian, you're in grave danger of missing the point of the Sermon on the Mount entirely. Familiarity with truth can be like an inoculation against its power. We've had a low dose of the Sermon on the Mount for so long that we are immune to the full-strength version. As you read Jesus' Sermon on the Mount (Matthew 5-7), I encourage you to read it with new eyes and with open ears. Read it out loud. Read it in a new translation. Write about it in a journal. Compose a poem. Talk about it in your family and small group gatherings.

Try to hear it as you might if you had been in the crowds that listened to these words from Jesus' own lips. Let its radicalness shame you and enflame you. Let its values implant themselves in your own soul. Allow it to weed the garden of your character and habits. Allow Jesus to transform you by the washing of his word.

If you are not yet a Christian, or perhaps tentatively re-seeking your own faith roots, let this Sermon on the Mount be an introduction for you to the real Jesus. You'll find his words both challenging and humbling. Realize that he is calling you to follow him on a journey. I encourage you to pray at the outset and say something like this:

> "Jesus, I'm going to be reading your words and trying to understand your thoughts. Guide my mind. But especially, change my heart and will. I can't be or live like the Sermon on the Mount indicates the way I am right now. You help me. You make it possible by your own Spirit. Reveal yourself to me. Amen."

Then stand back and watch out!

If you give this kind of active permission for God to work in you, he'll begin to do just that. Jesus will begin to become very real to you, kind of like a personal Friend and Guide through life's twists and turns. Not a buddy, but a Leader who knows you and loves you as an individual. I know this may sound strange, but give him a chance to reveal himself to you. The one who spoke these life-challenging words we call the Sermon on the Mount is also able to help you to experience their fulfillment in your own life.

Jesus is forming a people today, a band of radical followers who refuse to insulate themselves from his words and demands by the padding of a comfortable religion, a Christian counter-culture that challenges the present world order. Jesus is calling you.

You're invited.

Dr. Ralph F. Wilson
Loomis, California
December 24, 2007

Table of Contents

Reprint Guidelines

Copying the Handouts. In some cases, small groups or Sunday school classes would like to use these notes to study this material. That's great. An appendix provides copies of handouts designed for classes and small groups. There is no charge whatsoever to print out as many copies of the handouts as you need for participants.

www.jesuswalk.com/manifesto/manifesto-lesson-handouts.pdf

All charts and notes are copyrighted and must bear the line:

"Copyright © 2011, Ralph F. Wilson. All rights reserved. Reprinted by permission."

You may not resell these notes to other groups or individuals outside your congregation. You may, however, charge people in your group enough to cover your copying costs.

Copying the book (or the majority of it) in your congregation or group, you are requested to purchase a reprint license for each book. A Reprint License, $2.50 for each copy is available for purchase at

www.jesuswalk.com/books/manifesto.htm

Or you may send a check to:

Dr. Ralph F. Wilson
JesusWalk Publications
PO Box 565
Loomis, CA 95650, USA

The Scripture says,

"The laborer is worthy of his hire" (Luke 10:7) and "Anyone who receives instruction in the word must share all good things with his instructor." (Galatians 6:6)

However, if you are from a third world country or an area where it is difficult to transmit money, please make a small contribution instead to help the poor in your community.

References and Abbreviations

BDAG *A Greek-English Lexicon of the New Testament and Other Early Christian Literature*, by Walter Bauer and Frederick William Danker, (Third Edition; based on previous English editions by W.F. Arndt, F.W. Gingrich, and F.W. Danker; University of Chicago Press, 1957, 1979, 2000)

Cole R. Alan Cole, *The Epistle of Paul to the Galatians* (Tyndale New Testament Commentaries; Eerdmans, 1965)

Dana and Mantey H. E. Dana and Julius R. Mantey, *A Manual Grammar of the Greek New Testament* (Macmillan, 1927, 1955).

DJG Joel B. Green, Scot McKnight, I. Howard Marshall (Editors), *Dictionary of Jesus and the Gospels* (InterVarsity Press, 1992)

ISBE *The International Standard Bible Encyclopedia*, Geoffrey W. Bromiley (general editor), (Eerdmans, 1979-1988; fully revised from the 1915 edition)

France R.T. France, *The Gospel of Matthew* (New International Commentary on the New Testament; Eerdmans, 2007)

Jeremias Joachim Jeremias, *Jerusalem in the Time of Jesus* (Fortress Press, 1969, reprinted 1979)

Liddell-Scott Henry George Liddell. Robert Scott, *A Greek-English Lexicon* (revised and augmented throughout by Sir Henry Stuart Jones with the assistance of. Roderick McKenzie; Oxford, Clarendon Press, 1940, Perseus Project online edition)

Metzger Bruce M. Metzger, *A Textual Commentary on the Greek New Testament* (United Bible Societies, 1971)

Morris Leon Morris, *The Gospel According to Matthew* (Pillar Commentary series; Eerdmans, 1992)

NIDNTT *New International Dictionary of New Testament Theology*, Colin Brown (editor; Zondervan, 1975-1978; translated with additions and revisions from *Theologisches Begriffslexikon zum Neuen Testament*, Coenen, Beyreuther, and Bitenhard, editors)

Robertson Archibald Thomas Robertson, *Word Pictures in the New Testament* (Sunday

School Board of the Southern Baptist Convention, 1932, 1960)

Stott   John R.W. Stott, *The Message of the Sermon on the Mount* (InterVarsity Press, 1978)

TDNT   *Theological Dictionary of the New Testament*, Gerhard Kittel and Gerhard Friedrich (editors), Geoffrey W. Bromiley (translator and editor), (Eerdmans, 1964-1976; translated from *Theologisches Wörterbuch zum Neuen Testament*, ten volume edition). CD-ROM

Willard   Dallas Willard, *The Divine Conspiracy: Rediscovering Our Hidden Life in God* (HarperSanFrancisco, 1998)

Introduction to the Sermon on the Mount

Jesus comes preaching, "Repent, for the kingdom of God is at hand" (Matthew 4:17), that is, "Turn from your shallowness and sins. Change your hearts and your ways, and turn to God. For God's Kingdom is near, it is now, it breaking in upon you even as I speak."

What Is Righteousness?

Change? Change to what? What does a truly righteous person look like?

Henrik Olrik (1830-1890), "Sermon on the Mount" (1880), altarpiece, St. Matthew's Church, Copenhagen, Denmark

Not like the Pharisees of Jesus' day who claimed righteous conformance to Moses' law. Like Christian legalists of our own time, they went far beyond the Bible to a series of precautionary rules that put a hedge or fence around the law, lest they break it. Oh, these ancient and modern-day legalists are zealous, all right. But their hearts are essentially selfish, absorbed in their own righteous doing.

So what does Jesus have in mind when he calls for repentance and change? Something radically different than the religions of his age or ours. What he begins to teach his followers is not a formalized religion, really. Jesus teaches a new heart attitude towards God and people. An attitude that runs counter to human nature.

An Unattainable Ideal?

If you've read the Sermon on the Mount with any degree of self-examination, you come to realize that the quality of righteousness Jesus is talking about is far beyond yours and mine. It isn't about rules or a kind of wishy-washy love for mankind. It is about an attitude of heart that eludes us.

"Be perfect," Jesus taught, "as your heavenly Father is perfect."

Perfect? we ask. How can anyone be perfect?

And so we relegate the Sermon on the Mount to a great ideal to which we aspire on a good day. We make it a kind of hypothetical standard that none can attain but all acknowledge as a model.

Radical Alternative to Modern Values

But not all would agree with this standard. Not the cynical, secular world. Poor in spirit? Bah, humbug! Meek? No, a ruthless climbing-the-ladder-of-success-no-matter-what-the-cost is the religion of many. Pure in heart? Thirsting for righteousness? Our generation is embarrassed by such naiveté.

Our world tells us to invest for the future, to command the highest salary we can, and to accumulate wealth. Jesus tells us not to store up treasures on earth lest we make money our God. He tells us not to obsess over making a living, but to seek first his kingdom and his righteousness.

We build great institutions by naming buildings after the big donors, and putting little donors' names on pretentious plaques. Jesus says that when we give we are to do it secretly, anonymously.

Modern-day tolerance tells us all will find their way into God's presence some day, that many roads and religions lead to the Creator. But this radical Teacher from Galilee says that the gate to his kingdom is a small one, and the alternative road is broad and well-traveled and leads to destruction. Talk about narrow, exclusive thinking!

Christian Counter-Culture

You see, what Jesus is teaching in the Sermon on the Mount isn't warmed over religion. It is a call to a radical change. A change in attitude and heart. A change in values and lifestyle.

Preacher-scholar John Stott writes that the Sermon on the Mount:

> "… Is the nearest thing to a manifesto that [Jesus] ever uttered, for it is his own description of what he wanted his followers to be and to do. To my mind, no two words sum up its intention better, or indicate more clearly its challenge to the modern world, than the expression 'Christian counter-culture.'"[1]

---

[1] Stott, *Sermon,* p. 15.

Pipe-Dream or Possibility?

When we consider the practicality of the Sermon on the Mount, commentators are divided. There are several views:

1. **Unattainable and unpractical, though noble**. The unpragmatic idealism of a visionary, a dream without fulfillment. (Many commentators)

2. **An eschatological ethic**, capable of fulfillment only in the Age to Come (Dibelius). "Eschatological" means "concerning the Last Days" or "end times."

3. **An interim ethic** by a deluded prophet designed to prepare his followers for the end of history, a kind of martial law, not an ethic for every day. (Schweitzer, et al.)

4. **The constitution of the future millennial kingdom** in which Jews will live, the law of Moses raised to the nth power. It is not a law in effect now, and is not binding on Christians. (Classic Dispensationalism)

5. **Self-evidently true, common to all religions** and easy to follow. (A superficial view of those who haven't read it carefully)

6. **A way of life made possible only by a new heart**, brought about by a spiritual birth.

It is this last view that I hold. Jesus was teaching his followers a new way of life, a kingdom way of life that is only possible by the Spirit, with which he himself would baptize the Church.

Form and Structure of the Sermon on the Mount

A great deal of energy has been expended in the last 150 years to figure out the origins of the Gospels, and the Sermon on the Mount in particular. Are these the actual words Jesus spoke in a single sermon on a single occasion? Or are they a compilation and condensation of his teaching? Or are these Jesus' words at all? Are they perhaps merely words his disciples put in his mouth decades after his death?

We're not going to spend much time exploring these kinds of questions. First of all, they are highly speculative. Many scholars have become so distracted in dissecting the form and discerning the origins of Jesus' words, that they have neglected to teach them with conviction and passion. We cannot afford such a tragic mistake.

But I think it will be useful to frame some answers to the most common questions that a study of the Sermon on the Mount may raise:

1. Why are these teachings found in different contexts in other gospels? What is

their original form?

2.   Are these Jesus' actual words?

Let's briefly explore these questions.

The Synoptic Problem

Even a casual reader will notice that the first three gospels – Matthew, Mark, and Luke – have many verbal similarities, while the fourth gospel seems quite different. Because they have so much common material, the first three gospels are termed the Synoptic Gospels. The word "synoptic" comes from two Greek words *syn-*, "together" and *opsesthai*, "to see." It means "presenting or taking the same or common view."

Scholars have hypothesized, rightly, I believe, that the writers of the Synoptic Gospels must have had some common source document available to them that contained the stories and teachings of Jesus, some kind of proto-gospel. Scholars have a name for this hypothetical source; they call it Q, which stands for the German word *Quelle*, meaning "source."

The gospel writers, I assume, probably drew on Q and wove it together with their own eyewitness and other traditions to fashion an account of Jesus' life and teachings for their particular audience. Mark's gospel is commonly agreed to be the earliest gospel. Matthew's gospel seems to be written especially with Palestinian Jews in mind, and takes special care to point out Jesus' words and actions as the fulfillment of Old Testament prophecies. Luke's gospel seems to speak to a Hellenistic audience. The Gospel of John, on the other hand, didn't seem to use this Q source at all. As an eyewitness, John wrote from his own mature perspective of what Jesus said and did and intended. This is how I understand the relationship between the gospels.

Differences in Words and Setting

But what do we make of instances where one gospel says something in one way and another says it in altogether different way? Did Jesus really say both things? Or did the gospel writers take liberties with what he said and alter it to suit their own points of view, as some allege?

Let's consider Jesus' mission, for a moment. He was an itinerant teacher, traveling up and down the land of Palestine, teaching in scores of towns and villages over a period of perhaps three years.

If you've ever been on a speaking tour, you soon learn to refine and hone your main speech or series of speeches to a fine point. You learn what works and gets an audience response, and are sure to include those elements at the next stop on your tour. But you also find, if you speak without a manuscript (as Jesus surely did), that your core message gets expressed in various ways. Yes, you use many of the same illustrations, but with a particular audience you may emphasize a point that you don't develop with another audience. Your presentation may be similar, but never the same. And you continually find fresh ways to express your thoughts as your speak them.

Now, I don't mean to make Jesus out to be a speaker who played to the crowds or improved his message as he went along. His thoughts were unique and distinctive, and his words came from the Father for whom he spoke. But that doesn't mean that he spoke exactly the same words by rote in each town and hamlet. His expression varied.

Thus in Matthew, for example, the Beatitudes take the form of a series of single blessings:

> "Blessed are those who mourn,
> for they will be comforted." (Matthew 5:4)

While in Luke, we see a contrast of blessings with woes:

> "Blessed are you who weep now,
> for you will laugh...." (Luke 6:21b)

> "Woe to you who laugh now,
> for you will mourn and weep." (Luke 6:25b)

Which is the original? Which best represents Jesus' actual words? Why, both, of course. If we limit Jesus' true expression to a single Q source, we don't allow for the full expression of a Teacher who taught on perhaps a thousand occasions in his ministry.

I've doubtless oversimplified the Synoptic Problem. There are many unanswered questions. But my interest is in the words of Jesus that have come down to us in the New Testament canon, not trying to reconstruct some Q document that is not, and may never have been, in existence. I want to concentrate on Jesus' words that we have before us, and seek to understand them as they are written in one of the gospels – in the case of the Sermon on the Mount, in Matthew's Gospel.

The Jesus Seminar

Since 1985 we have been treated to the Jesus Seminar. It has been made up of a group of liberal scholars who voted on each passage in the gospels concerning the relative probability that a particular passage was Jesus' own words, or the words of a later disciple or editor. They voted with one of four colored beads. A red bead indicated that "Jesus surely said this." Pink meant, "He probably said that." Gray: "He probably didn't say this." Black: "It is very unlikely that he said anything like that."

How did they determine authenticity? The criterion of dissimilarity from his Jewish historical situation and from the early church, was one. But that is a judge of distinctiveness, not of authenticity. Next, they assumed that Jesus' sayings must be regarded as inauthentic unless they can be proved authentic. A strange assumption, it seems: guilty until proven innocent. They also apparently used the hypothetical Q source (which we don't have) and the supposedly-early Gospel of Thomas (which shows strong Gnostic influences and is probably second century) as the standard by which a saying was considered authentic. In the end, the Jesus Seminar concluded that as much as 82% of the gospels were invented by the early church, and weren't Jesus' words at all. Only a very few sayings and parables met the "red bead" standard.[2]

I've read enough of this sort of pseudo-scientific speculation to reject it as the refuse of unbelief.

But Are These Jesus' Actual Words?

If you were to read the Sermon on the Mount out loud it might take you all of fifteen minutes. I find it hard to believe that Jesus uttered just these words for a fifteen minute sermon, had the choir sing a hymn, gave a benediction, and then sent people home.

I think what we have in the Sermon on the Mount is some kind of synopsis of Jesus' teaching on a particular occasion, or perhaps of his core teaching. I believe that when these words were spoken, they were amplified with stories and parables suited to the audience.

Were these Jesus' actual words? Yes, I believe so. They weren't *all* that he said on this occasion, but I believe that he *did* say these things.

Of course, Jesus taught in Aramaic, a language closely related to Hebrew. The words as we have them are Greek, and finally we read them in an English translation of the Greek. While we may lose something in the translation, I believe that the text that we have is trustworthy and powerful – even in English!

Yes, Jesus actually said these things, and says them afresh to us today!

Is the Sermon on the Mount a Single Unit?

The text of Matthew 5-7 seems to be a single literary unit, intended for us to under-

---

[2] See the analysis by Ben Witherington III, *The Jesus Quest: The Third Search for the Jew of Nazareth* (Second Edition; InterVarsity Press, 1995, 1997), especially chapter 2.

stand as a teaching that begins with Jesus sitting down before the crowds on the mountainside in 5:1-2, and ending with Jesus finishing, leaving the listeners amazed at the boldness and authority of his words in 7:28-29.

But did Jesus actually speak all of these things at a single sitting? There's so much there, so much that is deep and pithy.

Yes, I believe it is quite possible. Jesus was not bound by the American church 20-minute sermon rule. He probably taught the assembled crowds for hours at a time, and they followed his words with rapt attention. What he was saying was not like any other rabbi or teacher. He spoke with a singular authority they found fascinating and wonderfully attractive.

Outline

In outlining the Sermon on the Mount, I found that it falls easily into several themes:

1. The character of Kingdom citizens (5:1-16)
2. The true spirit and intent of the law (5:17-48)
3. The nature of true piety (6:1-18)
4. The dangers of materialism (6:19-34)
5. True discernment (7:1-29)

For the most part, these themes seem to flow from one to another. The themes of the following section often grow out of seeds found in the previous section. Only the last section, which I have termed "True Discernment" seems a stretch; the other themes hold together very well and seem to have an inner unity, as well as a unity with each other.

Conclusion

I don't find it at all difficult to believe that Jesus delivered this teaching on a single occasion on a mountainside in Galilee. Why not?

Did he say more on that occasion? I have no doubt. Perhaps we have the "Cliff Notes" version of Jesus' extended discourse. Did he express these truths in somewhat different ways on other occasions throughout his ministry? Certainly. But I believe that what we have is accurate and authoritative on its own.

I invite you to read and study Jesus' words, not as a form-critical scholar but as a listener, a learner, a disciple, a would-be follower. Don't suspend your critical faculties, but use your energy to understand Jesus' meaning and how to apply its truths to your own life. Jesus surely spoke these powerful words, not to titillate modern scholars and provide grist for academic careers and learned books, but to lay out the radical shape of his Kingdom and to invite men and women to follow him. To that end I invite you, too, to join him – and me – in this awesome journey.

I. Kingdom Citizens (Matthew 5:1-16)

Citizens of the Kingdom of Heaven are different. They are gentle people, persisting people, witnessing people. We explore Jesus' teachings in this section in two chapters.

1. The Beatitudes (5:1-12)
2. Witnessing People: Living as Salt and Light in the World (5:13-16)

John Gibson (1790-1866), " Blessed are they that mourn for they shall be comforted," pen and brown ink with wash over pencil on wove paper, Royal Academy of Arts, London.

1. Paradoxical People: The Beatitudes (5:1-12)

"[1] Now when he saw the crowds, he went up on a mountainside and sat down. His disciples came to him, [2] and he began to teach them...." (5:1-2)

In our day teachers stand to teach, but in Jesus' day the rabbis sat, and Jesus followed in this great tradition. Crowds of eager listeners were following him, and so he sought a site that they could hear him well. Tradition places the Sermon on the Mount on a gentle hill between Capernaum and Tabgha, at the north end of the Sea of Galilee. Jesus would have had the beauty of this inland lake behind him as he taught, but all eyes

The location of the Sermon on the Mount is unknown, but tradition places it on the Mount of Beatitudes, at the north end of the Sea of Galilee. This is also the location of the Roman Catholic Church of the Beatitudes, built in 1938. Photo: Tor Hutchins. Used by permission.

were on him. Because Jesus spoke like no one they had ever heard.

Dallas Willard calls the Beatitudes of Jesus

"... among the literary and religious treasures of the human race ... acknowledged by almost everyone to be among the highest expressions of religious insight and moral inspiration."[1]

That afternoon, if afternoon it was, the hushed multitudes heard the religion of their world turned right side up for the first time in their lives. They heard something radically different than the Pharisees or scribes or anyone else was saying.

Jesus began to speak in paradoxes, in riddles, as wisdom was sometimes transmitted in ancient times. He called the poor rich, the mourners comforted, the meek as heirs of the entire earth. People listened. And as they listened they heard Jesus expound the character traits of the citizens of his new Kingdom.

Let's examine what he said and contrast it to the accepted wisdom of our own day.

[1] Willard, *Divine Conspiracy*, p. 98.

Blessed are the poor in spirit (5:3)

"Blessed are the poor in spirit, for theirs is the kingdom of heaven." (5:3)

Who are the poor in spirit? Certainly not the religious leaders. They were filled with a kind of haughty superiority over the common people. But Jesus is saying that those who aren't puffed up with their own spiritual superiority are the real possessors of the kingdom – the spiritual zeroes, those who have struggled with life and have come up short. They are the heirs of the kingdom. (See Excursus 1, "What Is the Kingdom of Heaven?" that follows.)

Jesus' mission was "to bring good news to the poor ... to proclaim freedom for the prisoners and recovery of sight for the blind, to release the oppressed" (Luke 4:18). The good news, the really excellent news he proclaimed was that the kingdom was not for the morally superior but for the poor in spirit. A physician doesn't come to make the healthy well, but for those who are sick (Matthew 9:12). Jesus came for those who were aware of their own spiritual poverty and hungry for more.

Blessed

What did Jesus mean when he said "Blessed are the ..."? The idea of blessing has a long and rich tradition in the Old Testament. The blessings of God begin in Genesis where God blesses the animals, and then man, saying, "Be fruitful and increase in number; fill the earth and subdue it..." (Genesis 1:28).

The Hebrew equivalent is *bārak*, which occurs 415 times in the Old Testament. To bless in the Old Testament means "to endue with power for success, prosperity, fecundity, longevity, etc."[2] The idea is of conferring or imparting something. Often this is done through the laying on of hands or the lifting of hands.[3] Jesus blesses the little children, his disciples, and his Father in heaven.

The word "Beatitude" comes from the Latin root *beatus*, "happy," from the past participle of Latin *beare*, "to bless." So the word "The Beatitudes" means "The Blessings." It is only a happy coincidence of the English language that the idea of "be-attitudes" or "attitudes of being" is suggested by the word Beatitude.

In the Beatitudes Jesus explains just who are the recipients of God's blessing, that is, his favor and grace. Not those whom the world sees as successful, but those whose spirits yearn for God. They are the truly blessed ones, and the extent of their blessedness

---

[2] John N. Oswalt, *bārak*, TWOT #285.
[3] See my article on "Lifting Hands in Worship," *Paraclete*, Winter 1986, pp. 4-8 (www.joyfulheart.com/scholar/hands.htm).

will become fully apparent at the end of the age when the superficiality of the world's standards will be exposed for what it is, and when those whose hearts belong to God are honored and judged righteous in his kingdom.

Jesus' first Beatitude is a paradox then. "How can the poor in spirit possess the kingdom?" is the riddle. The answer is this: Only those who are aware of their spiritual poverty will be seeking more. And those who seek the riches of Christ will possess his kingdom. You see this same theme in those who mourn, are meek, and who hunger and thirst for righteousness.

Q1. (Matthew 5:3-11) Each Beatitude consists of two parts. What are these parts? Why do you think Jesus made each Beatitude a paradox? What is the relationship of the Beatitudes to the Fruit of the Spirit (Galatians 5:22-23)?
http://www.joyfulheart.com/forums/index.php?showtopic=729

Blessed are those who mourn (5:4)

"Blessed are those who mourn, for they will be comforted."(5:4)

Here's another riddle: How can those who mourn be comforted? Who is mourning? The poor in spirit. Those who feel distanced from God. The hurt and oppressed. The ones in pain who feel alone. They mourn. And Jesus offers them comfort, comfort with his own blessing and warmth and healing and salvation.

But sometimes believers mourn, too. Jesus mourned over the fate of those who turn away from him to their own empty philosophies of life.

"O Jerusalem, Jerusalem, you who kill the prophets and stone those sent to you, how often I have longed to gather your children together, as a hen gathers her chicks under her wings, but you were not willing. Look, your house is left to you desolate." (Matthew 23:37-38)

We mourn when we see degradation and unrighteousness and injustice around us. We cannot afford to become inured to it, or accepting of sin. We must grieve inwardly or be untrue to the values of our Master. Ezekiel's vision recalls God's command to a man clothed in linen with a writing kit at his side:

"Go throughout the city of Jerusalem and put a mark on the foreheads of those who grieve and lament over all the detestable things that are done in it." (Ezekiel 9:3-4)

Sometimes we weep over the delay in justice, as did the martyrs in John's Revelation:

"How long, Sovereign Lord, holy and true, until you judge the inhabitants of the earth and avenge our blood?" (Rev. 6:10)

But the ultimate and final comfort will come at the end. We are given this promise, and this promise we hold onto:

> "He will wipe every tear from their eyes. There will be no more death or mourning or crying or pain, for the old order of things has passed away. I am making everything new!" (Revelation 21:4-5)

What is the answer to this riddle of the mourners being blessed by comfort? We mourn in our emptiness and purposelessness and pain, and are comforted by Jesus' salvation and the presence of his Spirit. We mourn with Jesus, too, and are comforted by his Return and the consummation of his Reign.

Q2. (Matthew 5:3-4) Why is it necessary to be aware of your spiritual poverty before you can become a Christian? What kind of mourning is necessary for a person to become a Christian? What kind of mourning is a common experience of Christians? (See Isaiah 61:2-3; Ezekiel 9:4.)

http://www.joyfulheart.com/forums/index.php?showtopic=730

Blessed are the meek (5:5)

> "Blessed are the meek, for they will inherit the earth." (5:5)

Few hymnals today include Charles Wesley's famous song,

> "Gentle Jesus meek and mild,
> Look upon a little child
> Pity my simplicity,
> Teach me, Lord, to come to Thee."[4]

But it seems to reflect a common view of Jesus and Christians. In a word: wimpy. Blessed are the wimpy, for they will inherit the earth? I don't think so.

The word translated "meek" is Greek *praüs*, meaning "'pertaining to not being overly impressed by a sense of one's self-importance, gentle, humble, considerate, meek' in the older favorable sense."[5] This is confusing for us, since English has two definitions for "meek": (1) "enduring injury with patience and without resentment, mild," and (2) "deficient in spirit and courage, submissive."

---

[4] Charles Wesley, *Hymns and Sacred Poems* (1742).
[5] *Praüs*, BDAG 861.

Jesus didn't mean "blessed are the deficient in courage." Rather, he meant "enduring injury with patience and without resentment." Jesus uses the word *praüs* to describe himself in Matthew 11:29: "... For I am gentle (NIV; KJV "meek") and humble in heart, and you will find rest for your souls." Do you see Jesus as lacking courage? Is he submissive to those who tried to shut him up? No.

But Jesus was gentle, humble, and considerate. He cared about people and the way he treated them reflected this love. In Paul's list of the fruit of the Spirit (Galatians 5:22-23), we see this quality in the character traits "patience, kindness, goodness" and the word itself is used: "gentleness" (NIV) or "meekness" (KJV).

But those in the world who want to make something of themselves don't value meekness. Instead they push themselves in front of others, promote themselves, and climb the ladder to success over the bodies of their fellows. Get ahead, that's the way to inherit the earth.

And herein lies the paradox. The meek, not the proud, will inherit the earth. That is because the King embodies love at its highest, courage at its greatest, humbling himself to the lowest, in order to save to the uttermost those who are lost.

The world doesn't understand such a King, nor does it understand Jesus. It is attracted to Jesus, but it finally rejects his way as impractical. "I'll do it myself," they promise. "I'll pull myself up by my own bootstraps. I'll be captain of my soul, and no one will tell me what to do." The antithesis of meekness. And here is the riddle. Those who trust in themselves rather than God will be left with nothing, blessing-less, while the meek, the humble, the trusters-in-God, will inherit the earth and God's blessing. How much we actually believe this will be clearly reflected in the decisions we make and in the way we live.

Q3. (Matthew 5:5) How does this sort of gentleness contrast with the world's ideal? How is humility important to Christlikeness?
http://www.joyfulheart.com/forums/index.php?showtopic=731

Blessed are the hungry for righteousness (5:6)

"Blessed are those who hunger and thirst for righteousness, for they will be filled." (5:6)

A fourth characteristic of citizens of the Kingdom is an intense hunger and thirst for righteousness. What kind of righteousness? Moral perfection? That doesn't exist this side of heaven, does it? What kind of a silly pie-in-the-sky attitude on which to base one's life! Real success comes from a situational ethics which bends when it needs to in order to reach goals that are important. That's the way to the top.

"No wide-eyed, eager, wholesome, innocent Sunday school teacher for me. No sir!" says Professor Harold Hill in *"The Music Man."* The world makes fun of those who desire to do what is right, to tell the truth, to seek real justice. Those whose ideals get in the way of success are mocked. Those who refuse to compromise, even to their detriment, are scorned.

But the way to heaven is not the same path as the road to worldly success. Jesus offers a blessing to those who seek righteousness with all their heart, who thirst for it. And he promises that they will be filled with it.

What a strange and wonderful promise: Those who seek righteousness will find it; those who thirst for righteousness will be filled to the brim with it.

The fulfillment of this blessing, of course, is not by human effort. That was epitomized by the law-keeping of the Pharisees that failed to touch the human heart. The fulfillment, of course, is the blessing of the Kingdom itself, the presence and powerful working of God's Spirit within his people.

You may hate yourself for your sin and long to be righteous. Desire it, ache for it. And Jesus promises you that you will receive that righteousness. What a blessing! It is a costly blessing, to be sure. The way God extends this righteousness to you is by offering you his own in exchange for yours:

> "For Christ died for sins once for all, the righteous for the unrighteous, to bring you to God." (1 Peter 3:18)

How can those who despise true righteousness receive this blessing? This Beatitude, like the others, requires a change of heart to receive it.

Q4. (Matthew 5:6) How can an intense desire for righteousness put you at odds with the world? What sort of righteousness is Jesus talking about, do you think? What promise are we given in this Beatitude?
http://www.joyfulheart.com/forums/index.php?showtopic=732

Blessed are the merciful (5:7)

> "Blessed are the merciful, for they will be shown mercy." (5:7)

On January 26, 1999 in St. Louis, Pope John Paul II entreated the Governor of Missouri, Mel Carnahan, a Baptist, to spare the life of a convicted triple murderer. Not because he was innocent, the Pope argued, but because "the dignity of human life must never be taken away, even in the case of someone who has done great evil." The Governor commuted the sentence in deference to this man of God.

While I might disagree with the Pope on capital punishment, my heart is with him in extending mercy, for he represents a Christ celebrated not for harshness and vindictiveness, but for mercy. On the cross, Jesus prayed, "Forgive them, Father, for they know not what they do" (Luke 23:34). Could you or I have said that? Could we have felt it *and* said it? Jesus did. In Pilate he saw the extremity of grasping – selfish power grasping. In the Pharisees he observed a pious hypocrisy and in the soldiers the callous disregard for human life – men who crucified him and then gambled for his clothing as he hung gasping for breath above them on the cross. Above all that pettiness and evil he extended forgiveness.

The powers that be in this world do not admire mercy. They admire passionless, difficult decisions that get the job done. They admire ruthlessness. And if they don't really admire it in others, they excuse their own practice of it as a show of strength of character and resolve.

Do we Christians really love mercy? Don't we instead offer judgment in the place of love and condemnation in the place of grace? Showing mercy does not mean that we condone evil.

Seeking to expose Jesus' characteristic mercy, his enemies brought a trembling young woman, caught in the act of adultery, into the temple and flung her before Jesus. "Stone her," they shouted.

Jesus knelt and wrote in the dirt that covered the temple courtyard. Then he looked up and said, "Let him who is without sin cast the first stone." Soon, her accusers – and Jesus' accusers – had disappeared (John 7:53-8:11). His telling question struck them. They knew they had sinned; how could they condemn?

We believers know of our own sin, and that only God's mercy saves us, and so we extend this mercy to others. Mercy is a banner of glory. Mercy is a badge of honor. Mercy is good news to a guilt-ridden, neurotic world that desperately needs to hear one in Authority say, "Neither do I condemn you, go and sin no more" (John 8:11).

This kind of mercy scarcely fits the world's ideal of strength, no more than do the other Beatitudes. But in this riddle we find the gospel: "Blessed are the merciful, for they shall receive mercy." The merciful are the ones who are aware of their own need and of God's mercy to them. It is no wonder that Jesus incorporates this joining of mercy-giving and mercy-receiving into his model prayer: "Forgive us our debts, *as we have also forgiven our debtors*" (Matthew 6:12). Jesus' way knows nothing of condemning forgivees, only of forgiveness. In acting like God ourselves, we receive God's blessing.

Blessed are the pure in heart (5:8)

> "Blessed are the pure in heart, for they will see God." (5:8)

Is there any such thing as purity of heart? we ask. Perhaps in a young child. No, even babies learn in their infancy to manipulate and bend the wills of others to their way. Those who would be great have long since left purity of heart and departed with expediency on their arm. Is purity of heart even to be desired?

Yes. Yes, we must answer, when we look at Jesus. Purity of heart for him was not a naive ignorance of lust, corruption, and evil. He knew what it was: a single-eyed devotion to his Father. His purity consisted in serving his Father fully and always – purity of heart with courage, purity of heart when in danger for his life. We see purity of heart in Jesus.

Jesus' promise in this Beatitude is that the pure in heart will be blessed with the ability to see and know and discern God himself. Those whose lives are filled with compromise and conformity, lust and licentiousness cannot see God. They cannot know him.

None of us can, for that matter. Since we all have a flawed heart, we must reach out to God himself to purify our hearts and cleanse them.

When the prophet Isaiah was called in the year King Uzziah died, he says, "I saw the Lord, seated on a throne, high and lifted up, and the train of his robe filled the temple." He cries out, "Woe to me. I am ruined. For I am a man of unclean lips, and I live among a people of unclean lips, and my eyes have seen the King, the LORD Almighty."

Then he tells of an angel who brought a live coal from the altar, touched his lips with it, and said, "See, this has touched your lips; your guilt is taken away and your sin atoned for" (Isaiah 6:1-7).

God is able to purge the corruption of our hearts and make them pure again. And, like Isaiah, give us that holy vision of God. The Book of Revelation closes with the promise of intimacy with God: "They will see his face!" (Revelation 22:4).

And so purity of heart is an earmark of Jesus' disciples. Not perfection – yet. But hearts cleansed and made pure by Christ himself. And hearts that actively seek that purity that allows an intimacy with the Lord. Jesus' disciples are men and women, boys and girls, who prefer closeness to God to the allurements of sin. And he promises, "They will see God."

Q5. (Matthew 5:8) *Why* **can people with a pure heart see, know, and discern God? Why can't "chronic" sinners see God? How do we obtain the pure or clean heart that Jesus describes?**

http://www.joyfulheart.com/forums/index.php?showtopic=733

Blessed are the peacemakers (5:9)

"Blessed are the peacemakers, for they will be called sons of God." (5:9)

Jesus offers still another riddle about peacemakers. How can a peacemaker be called a son of God? he asks.

Picture in your mind a movie Western. On the porch in front of the Sheriff's office sits a lawman, caressing his six-shooter.

"What's that?" he's asked.

"Why that's my Peacemaker, son," he replies.

Strange, how our society seeks to twist peacemaking into violence. Peacemaking is always risky, never easy, and we shy away from it. The worldly wise never take the risks inherent with peacemaking. They reject the peace of sharing with the violence of taking, and forcing those around them into their own mold.

Police officers know that intervening in cases of domestic violence is the most dangerous part of their everyday responsibility. But they do it anyway and are known as Peace Officers. In 1995 Yitzhak Rabin, then Prime Minister of Israel, was murdered for peacemaking. He dared to extend his hand across the jagged breach between the embattled Israelis and the oppressed Palestinians, and he was killed for it by one of his own countrymen.

Peacemakers are an endangered breed. But Jesus says, cryptically, in this Beatitude, that "they will be called sons of God." Why? Because the Only Begotten Son of God, was the quintessential Peacemaker, the Prince of Peace, placing his own life in jeopardy to reconcile us to God. His hands were stretched out dangerously wide on the cross, his shoulders ached, as he held God's hand in one and man's hand in the other, and brought them together in his own body on the tree (1 Peter 2:24).

And so Jesus calls us, too, to be peacemakers, reconcilers. Yes, it will be costly. We will be misunderstood and despised by many. Jesus was. But we will be doing God's work and God will reward us.

And so Jesus' riddle about the messy task of peacemaking is answered in the profound promise, "they will be called sons of God." What a character profile to live up to!

Blessed are those who are persecuted (5:10-12)

"¹⁰ Blessed are those who are persecuted because of righteousness, for theirs is the kingdom of heaven.

¹¹Blessed are you when people insult you, persecute you and falsely say all kinds of evil against you because of me.

¹² Rejoice and be glad, because great is your reward in heaven, for in the same way they persecuted the prophets who were before you." (5:10-12)

Why are the Beatitudes so beloved if they are so difficult? Here's another riddle, harder to understand than those that preceded it: the persecuted are the blessed ones. This seems to run in the face of logic!

Yes, Jesus says. Though they are discriminated against and attacked by men, yet God will bless them for remaining true to the righteous living that they stand for. They refuse to back down in the face of threats because they are sold out to God and God will honor them for it. They may have earned the hatred and malice of men, but they have earned the favor of God himself for their courage and he will reward them with possession of the kingdom of heaven.

Sometimes it's difficult to see the glory in persecution. It is bigoted. It is ugly. It is unfair and unfounded. We suffer shame and pain for what we stand for and wonder if it is ultimately worth it. Yes, shouts Jesus, it *is* worth it. Look at it for what it is: The reward for conformity to the world's shabby political correctness is shame. And the reward for standing for righteousness is an eternal one. There is no comparing the two. How can we doubt? Yet sometimes we do. We begin to understand when we look at our Master who marked the path clearly before us.

"Let us fix our eyes on Jesus, the author and perfecter of our faith, who for the joy set before him endured the cross, scorning its shame, and sat down at the right hand of the throne of God. Consider him who endured such opposition from sinful men, so that you will not grow weary and lose heart" (Hebrews 12:2-3)

The Blessing of the Persecuted (5:10) moves quickly to the Blessing of Those who are Insulted and Falsely Maligned because of Jesus (5:11). This is probably an example of Hebrew parallelism, where verse 10 and verse 11 state the same truth in slightly different words.

Rejoicing in Persecution (5:12)

Jesus concludes this string of blessings with another amazing declaration:

"Rejoice and be glad, because great is your reward in heaven." (5:12)

How can we rejoice in the hot breath of slander? How can we be glad in the face of evil? By looking beyond it to the goal. Men and women of character have always done this. They have endured the pain of the moment for the fulfillment of the promise. I know that this is roundly derided as "pie in the sky when you die, by-and-by." But the principle of delayed gratification is grounded by experience in both the physical and spiritual realms.

Jesus tells us to look at what they are saying and laugh. Not at our tormentors, but in the glory of God that we anticipate. We are to laugh the laugh of faith. And now he tells us why. "For in the same way they persecuted the prophets who were before you." And in our pain we begin to understand.

We are blessed when we are persecuted, because persecution means that we have been seen. That we have been heard. That our actions have been taken note of by the powers that be and have made their mark. That we have done something right enough, for a change, to deserve persecution – something that puts us in the same class as the prophets whom Jesus so honored for their faith and courage. Something that puts us in the same class as Jesus himself, who suffered persecution.

What an audacious statement, that we might be in a class with Jesus himself! But that is the point of his statement. We are blessed when we are persecuted *in that* we receive a prophet's reward. No, we have not been elevated here by our own blind and selfish zeal. But by God's grace we are enabled to enjoy a wonderful privilege, to be counted among the choice ones of God. Paul was once a persecutor, but now he counted it an immense privilege to share in "the fellowship of Christ's sufferings" (Philippians 3:10), to "fill up in my flesh what is still lacking in regard to Christ's afflictions" (Colossians 1:24).

We in America are largely ignorant of this fellowship of Christ's sufferings. But our brothers and sisters in India and Saudi Arabia and China know that blessing and that fellowship, for they have not backed down in the face of persecution and insult, of threat, and of death itself.

Q6. (Matthew 5:10-12) Why should we rejoice when we are persecuted? What keeps this from being some kind of sick masochism, or finding pleasure in pain? Why is the blessing "for theirs is the kingdom of heaven" appropriate for the persecuted?
http://www.joyfulheart.com/forums/index.php?showtopic=734

The Beatitudes are from start to finish a riddle, a paradox, a series of riddles. The world admires them as great literature and as a statement of ideals held in honor, but denies the possibility of their actual fulfillment. It does not know the key to these Blessings.

The key to the riddle of the Blessings is found in the Holy Spirit whom Jesus gives to those who seek his forgiveness and pledge allegiance to him. For it is in this Spirit alone, not effort, even valiant effort by the best of people, that we can fulfill these Conditions and Blessings. But with the Spirit of Jesus within us, literally, we can and must live out these Beatitudes as a testimony to our world of the Living Christ. God grant us the surrender to Him and the teachability that can make it so. Amen.

Prayer

Father, give us the continual desire to seek you with all our hearts. Fill us with your Spirit. Build your character within us, so that you will be pleased and that these Conditions and Blessings may be fulfilled in us. In Jesus' name, we pray. Amen.

Excursus 1: What Is the Kingdom of Heaven that Jesus Proclaims?

Many centuries before Christ, when the nation of Israel was constituted on Mt. Sinai, the people accepted the Covenant of God their King.

> "Although the whole earth is mine, you will be for me a kingdom of priests and a holy nation." (Exodus 19:6)

A desert palace was made for the King called the tabernacle in the wilderness, his throne (the ark) was a gilded seat between two cherubim, and his presence was evidenced by a pillar of cloud by day and a pillar of fire by night. When he gave the orders to march the people broke camp, and when he signaled a halt they stopped again. They followed the King, his commands communicated through Moses, his prime minister.

Carl Heinrich Bloch (Danish painter, 1834-90), "Christ and Staff," oil on canvas.

But the people grew restive. "We want a king over us," they cried. "Then we will be like all other nations, with a king to lead us and to go out before us and fight our battles" (1 Samuel 8:19-20). God was displeased. "It is not you they have rejected," he told the prophet Samuel, "but they have rejected me as their king" (1 Samuel 8:7).

Nevertheless, the Lord acquiesced to their wishes and appointed a king for them. First, Saul, and when he proved unfit, David, who came from the tribe of Judah and was born in the village of Bethlehem. Note carefully that this was the Kingdom of God, not a human kingdom. Yes, David reigned, but he reigned for Yahweh the King as a kind of vice-regent. The prophet Nathan delivered to him an awesome promise:

> "Your house and your kingdom will endure forever before me; your throne will be established forever," and one of your sons will always sit upon it (2 Samuel 7:16).

Son of David, Messianic King

Jesus himself was that Son of David who had come to take up the Reign of God once more and restore the Kingdom to Israel. But it was not a kingdom with human glory like David's or Solomon's, but one with spiritual glory like the Kingdom in the Wilderness, where the King himself dwelt in the midst of his people. It is a spiritual kingdom which extends to every heart and life that acknowledges his kingship and obeys his commands.

So when Jesus came preaching, "Repent for the kingdom of heaven is near" (Matthew 4:17), he was speaking of himself. The kingdom was near in the King who was now in their midst. He proclaimed this truth to the Pharisees who surely did not have the kingdom in their hearts: "The kingdom of God is *in the midst of you.*" (Luke 17:21, RSV).[1]

This Reign of God, this Kingdom of God in the person of Christ, was resisted and rejected by the religious establishment, but received and embraced by the common folk, "the poor in spirit." Indeed, theirs *was* the kingdom.

Kingdom of Believers

The Kingdom once was the exclusive sphere of the Jews and those who joined themselves to them. But in one foreboding parable (Matthew 21:33-46), Jesus hints of a change. He tells of a landowner who plants a vineyard and then rents it out to tenants. When he sent his servants to collect the owner's share of the harvest, the tenants beat and killed them. Finally, the landowner sends his son to them, and they kill him, too. This is an allegory. The landowner is God, the vineyard his Kingdom, the tenants the Jews, the servants the prophets, and the son Jesus. In rejecting the King, the Jews have made themselves ineligible to be part of his Kingdom any longer. Jesus concludes the parable with the awesome words,

> "Therefore I tell you that the kingdom of God will be taken away from you and given to a people who will produce its fruit." (Matthew 21:43)

Now for a quick trip into the Letters of Paul to see the big picture. The physical Kingdom consisted of the descendents of the Twelve Tribes. The spiritual Kingdom consists of the spiritual descendents of the Twelve Apostles, "the Israel of God" (Galatians 6:16). While the Jews have been rejected (Romans 11) for now, "until the full number of the Gentiles has come in", then Israel will turn to the Lord and finally be included in the Kingdom and Jesus' salvation (Romans 11:26). Finally, Jesus will deliver the kingdom to his Father (1 Corinthians 15:24-28).

Various Christian groups have developed elaborate doctrines and timetables in which to fit these events. We will not venture yet another. God is the timekeeper, and will bring about all these things in the fullness of his time.

Kingdom of Heaven or Kingdom of God?

But what does the phrase "kingdom of heaven" mean? Is it the same as the phrase "kingdom of God"? I've heard a lot of theories, but when you compare Matthew's gospel with the many parallel passages in the other Synoptics, Mark and Luke, you find that where Matthew says "kingdom of heaven," Mark and Luke say "kingdom of God." The explanation is this: Matthew was writing especially for a Jewish audience who were careful not to utter the name of God, lest they be guilty of breaking the Third Commandment, "to take the name of the Lord your God in vain" (Exodus 20:7). We hear people doing the same thing today. "For heaven's sake!" someone will exclaim. They've trained themselves to speak that way so as not to dishonor God.

When you see "kingdom of heaven" in Matthew, it means exactly the same thing as "kingdom of God" in the other gospels. It refers to the Reign of God which has come in the person of Jesus Christ himself, and will culminate in the coming of Christ and his reign on earth, the time looked forward to in the Lord's Prayer: "Thy kingdom come, thy will be done, on earth as it is in heaven" (Matthew 6:10). The Kingdom is now in the presence of the King in our lives through his Spirit. Yet we look forward to the future when that "earnest of the Spirit" (KJV, 2 Corinthians 1:22; 5:5; Ephesians 1:14), that down payment we've received, will be completed when the King returns and establishes his kingdom on earth where there was once human resistance and rebellion.

References to the Kingdom in the Sermon on the Mount

"Blessed are the poor in spirit,
for theirs is the kingdom of heaven." (5:3)

"Blessed are those who are persecuted because of righteousness,
for theirs is the kingdom of heaven." (5:10)

"Anyone who breaks one of the least of these commandments and teaches others to do the same will be called least in the kingdom of heaven, but whoever practices and teaches these commands will be called great in the kingdom of heaven. For I tell you that unless your righteousness surpasses that of the Pharisees and the teachers of the law, you will certainly not enter the kingdom of heaven." (5:19-20)

"... Your kingdom come,
your will be done

on earth as it is in heaven." (6:10)

"But seek first his kingdom and his righteousness, and all these things will be given to you as well." (6:33)

"Not everyone who says to me, 'Lord, Lord,' will enter the kingdom of heaven, but only he who does the will of my Father who is in heaven." (7:21)

2. Witnessing People: Living as Salt and Light in the World (5:13-16)

Jesus' teaching on salt and light follows hard on the heels of the Beatitudes, which closes extolling the blessedness of those who are persecuted for Jesus' sake. Together, the Beatitudes and the Parables of Salt and Light form a kind of profile of the Spirit-filled disciple.

Some have been persecuted for silent protest. But many more have been vilified for declaring the Good News by both their deeds *and* their words. Jesus doesn't restrict our witness to words only or deeds only. Together they comprise the blessing of uncompromising witness.

Fra Angelico, "Sermon on the Mount" (1442), Museo Di San Marco Dell'Angelico, Florence.

In verses 13-16 Jesus tells two simple parables and draws conclusions from them. Using parables was a characteristic teaching method for Jesus. He chose two simple concepts – salt and light – and expounded from them principles for living.

Salty Christians (5:13a)

> "You are the salt of the earth. But if the salt loses its saltiness, how can it be made salty again? It is no longer good for anything, except to be thrown out and trampled by men." (5:13)

"Salty Christians" almost sounds like a serving of "fish and chips." Salty Christians, Jesus tells us emphatically, are much to be preferred over the salt-free variety.

A proper amount of salt (sodium chloride, NaCl) is essential to sustain life, so ancient peoples traded whatever was required to obtain it. In Palestine, most salt came from salt caves in the area around the Dead Sea. Both ancient and modern peoples have used salt as both (1) a food preservative (so Plutarch and Baruch 6:28), and (2) to bring out the flavor of foods (Job 6:6; Colossians 4:6). It was also used to make covenants and mixed with sacrifices.

Salt as a Preservative

So what does it mean to be the salt of the earth? If we use the preservative analogy, we would say that Christians by their very presence help preserve the world and hold back the wrath of God against it. I believe that God's mercy on our sinful world is due to the prayers and presence of the saints on earth. Abraham argued with God over the fate of Sodom and Gomorrah, "Will not the Judge of all the earth do right?" he asked. "Will you sweep away the righteous with the wicked?" And God answered, "For the sake of ten I will not destroy it" (Genesis 18:25, 23, 32).

But our presence is not only a shield against the wrath of God upon the earth. We also serve as those who by their wholesome presence bring about change and healing in a corrupt society. By the Eighteenth Century, England had sunk to a sad state. Gin flowed freely and drunkenness was common through all classes of society. Gambling was extremely popular, the clergy were corrupt and materialistic, and rationalism and deism held sway among the educated. Historians openly credit the Wesleyan Revival in England with saving society. It was the fearless preaching of John and Charles Wesley and George Whitfield that restored a conscience and brought people to a saving encounter with their God. To be sure, the Wesleys and Whitfield were mocked and vilified by the

"John Wesley" (1703-91), portrait by Nathaniel Hone (1766), oil on canvas, 49-1/2 x 39-1/4", National Portrait Gallery, London.

enemies of God. They were stoned and harassed and run out of town. But by their uncompromising witness, and that of their followers and lay preachers, England was saved and changed.

This awakened conscience was responsible for the final prohibition of the slave trade in England. This was cause championed by William Wilberforce, who had been led to Christ by former slave ship captain John Newton, author of the song "Amazing Grace." Christians *are* the salt of the earth. Their influence is wholesome and good and healing.

Who led the way toward the abolition of slavery in the United States? Christians. Who led the way toward a non-violent protest against racial discrimination? Christians. Who today stand for the life of the unborn child? Christians. Catholic Christians and Protestant Christians together. Yes, it is an embattled position, but it is right. And Christians can serve as the conscience of the nation today as they have in the past.

While it is true that ancient peoples used salt as a preservative, a search of the Bible for this use of salt comes up empty. The closest we come is a reference in the Apocrypha. The Epistle of Jeremiah speaks of women who preserve some of the meat sacrificed to idols:

> "As for the things that are sacrificed unto them, their priests sell and abuse; in like manner their wives lay up part thereof in salt; but unto the poor and impotent they give nothing of it." (part of Baruch 6:28)

The closest we come in the canonical scriptures was the use of salt to render land unusable (Judges 9:45), the rubbing of newborns with salt (to purify them? Ezekiel 16:4), or Elisha's use of salt to sweeten or purify a spring and remove its poison (2 Kings 2:20-21).

Salt as a Seasoning

There is much more evidence in the Bible of salt being used as seasoning, and in the parable we are studying, Jesus seems to be referring more to salt's taste than its effects.

Salt was used with sacrifices as a way of honoring the King to whom the sacrifices were made (Leviticus 2:13; Ezra 6:9; Ezekiel 43:24). Salt was used in the making of covenants (Numbers 18:19). We read of its ability to add flavor to food (Job 6:6), and Paul writes,

> "Let your conversation be always full of grace, seasoned with salt, so that you may know how to answer everyone" (Colossians 4:6).

Here, as in Jesus' parable of Christians being the salt of the earth, salt has to do with witness and conversation. In Colossians 4:6 it is used with the Greek word *artuō*, "to add condiments to something, to season, to salt."[1]

I believe that the primary meaning of "You are the salt of the earth" has to do with a willingness to live our lives with the "tang" of our faith intact. We're under so much pressure to give up our differences and blend in with society. Believers are to be "tangy" rather than bland and insipid in the way we live and speak.

---

[1] *Artuō*, BDAG 137.

Q1. (Matthew 5:13) In what sense are Christians the "salt of the earth" using the preservation analogy? In what sense are Christians the "salt of the earth" using the seasoning analogy?

http://www.joyfulheart.com/forums/index.php?showtopic=735

The salt the Israelites obtained was often impure, mixed with alkali salts from around the Dead Sea. Water could leach out the sodium chloride, leaving the other salts intact, so that it looked like salt but tasted insipid. This seems to be the basis of Jesus' warning about salt losing its saltiness. The essential Christ-inspired difference in our lives can be leached out by the constant flow of the world's values through our lives.[2]

We can come to the point where we have given up our standards and now stand for nothing. We may disguise it by saying that the zeal of youth has been tempered with the wisdom of maturity, but that is only a partial excuse. Someone once phrased the issue this way: If you were being tried for being for being a Christian, would there be enough evidence to convict you?

If we no longer stand boldly and faithfully for Christ and Christian values, we become worthless to him. Less than worthless, in fact, since by our mild claims of our Christianity we act as a counterfeit of the real salt. Worthless, insipid, tangy-less salt is good for nothing except for throwing on the pathway to keep the grass from growing on it. Would you rather be a grass killer or a food enhancer?

Q2. (Matthew 5:13) What might be the symptoms of a Christian who has lost his "saltiness"? Is it possible for a believer to detect such symptoms in himself or herself? What do secular people notice about a "de-saltified" Christian? What do other Christians notice about you? Is it possible to "resaltify" your life?

http://www.joyfulheart.com/forums/index.php?showtopic=736

The Light of the World (5:14-16)

"You are the light of the world. A city on a hill cannot be hidden. Neither do people light a lamp and put it under a bowl. Instead they put it on its stand, and it gives light to everyone in the house." (5:14-15)

[2] Friedrich Hauck, *halas*, in TDNT 1:228-229; William Barclay, *The Gospel of Matthew*, volume 1, p. 115.

Jesus' second parable about uncompromising witness has to do with light. In Jesus' day, homes were commonly lit by small clay lamps which could be held in the palm of the hand. The most primitive consisted of a saucer to hold the olive oil, in which was immersed one end of a wick that lay in an indentation or spout in the rim. Later clay lamps were sometimes covered, with a hole in the top in which to pour the oil, and a hole at one side for the wick. Don't be confused by the KJV translation of Greek *lychnos*, "lamp," as "candle." This tends to mislead modern ears, since "candle" suggests to us long wax tapers with a wick protruding from the top. The word is best translated "lamp."

In explaining the concept of making one's witness clear, Jesus introduces a third parable, "A city set on a hill cannot be hidden" (5:14b). Cities were usually situated on hilltops for protection against attack. It is much more difficult to storm a walled city running uphill, and defenders have always known that victory must be claimed by capturing and holding the high ground. Jesus' point, however, is not a city's defense, but its visibility because of its elevated position.

Byzantine period oil lamp, found in tomb in Samaria, village of Fandaqomiya (Pentacomia). Photo: Thameen Darby.

In the same way, he continues, a lampstand would elevate the lamp for greatest illumination within a room. Now he contrasts elevating a lamp on a lampstand to covering a lamp with a bowl. People don't light a lamp to hide its light under a bowl, Jesus says. That's silly! Rather people light a lamp in order to shed light to everyone in the house.

Q3. (Matthew 5:14-15) In the parable of "the light of the world," Jesus notes the stupidity of lights being hidden under bowls. Concerning what danger in the life of a Christian disciple does Jesus warn us in this parable?

http://www.joyfulheart.com/forums/index.php?showtopic=737

Evoking praise towards God (5:16)

"In the same way, let your light shine before men, that they may see your good deeds and praise your Father in heaven." (5:16)

Now Jesus comes to the point: letting people see your good works rather than hiding them. And here is the reason for a Christian's witness: "that [men] may see your good deeds and praise your Father in heaven."

Both salt and light are worthless if they are saltless or hidden from view. Jesus gives these parables right after a discussion of persecution. So we must be willing to bear our witness, even though it may bring persecution. Indeed, Paul says, "Everyone who wants to live a godly life in Christ Jesus will be persecuted" (2 Timothy 3:12). It comes with the territory.

They persecuted our Lord and Master, Jesus Christ. If our lives are becoming more and more like him it shouldn't surprise us if we are persecuted, too. And persecution should bring us joy, says Jesus, "for in the same way they persecuted the prophets who were before you" (Matthew 5:12). Persecution means that people see enough of Jesus in us to be worth resisting and persecuting, so we should count it as a badge of honor, and the portent of a great reward in heaven.

But our purpose in witness is never to stimulate persecution for the sake of reward. That would be essentially selfish. Rather it is to let our light shine so clearly that people can see God clearly in our works and in our deeds, and evoke praise to him.

Words versus deeds

Sometimes people place a false dichotomy between words and deeds. "I testify to my faith in God by the way I live," some say defiantly. "I don't have to say anything."

I agree that we *must* live lives that bring credit upon Jesus or our words won't be taken seriously. They will be laughed at as hypocrisy and thrown back in our face, and become a cause of greater unbelief on the part of those who watch us.

But deeds without words tell only half the story. Part of seasoning our conversation with salt (Colossians 4:6) is telling the good news to those around us. "The Word became flesh and dwelt among us, full of grace and truth" (John 1:14). Why is Jesus called "The Word"? Because he was the expression of his Father, and spoke the words his Father gave him to speak.

Our witness must consist of both deeds *and* words that point to God the Father and bring glory to him. What a privilege we have to be the agents of evoking praise to our Father in heaven!

Q4. (Matthew 5:13-15) How do verses 13-16 relate to verses 10-12? How does hiding our light affect the glory of God? Why must glory and suffering go hand in hand? Was Jesus' suffering necessary? Is ours? What does this have to do with Romans 12:2?
http://www.joyfulheart.com/forums/index.php?showtopic=738

A Light to the Nations

Through the prophet Isaiah, God begins to delineate the role and ministry of his people and servant Israel, and their embodiment in his Servant the Messiah.

> "It is too small a thing for you to be my servant
> to restore the tribes of Jacob
> and bring back those of Israel I have kept.
> I will also make you **a light for the Gentiles**,
> that you may bring my salvation to the ends of the earth" (Isaiah 49:6)

> "Listen to me, my people;
> hear me, my nation:
> The law will go out from me;
> my justice will become **a light to the nations**" (Isaiah 51:4)

> "Arise, shine, for your light has come,
> and the glory of the Lord rises upon you.
> See, darkness covers the earth
> and thick darkness is over the peoples,
> but the Lord rises upon you
> and his glory appears over you.
> **Nations will come to your light**,
> and kings to the brightness of your dawn" (Isaiah 60:1-3).

Where once this commission was given to the nation of Israel, it is now passed on to the citizens of the Kingdom of God as our commission, too (Acts 1:8). As Jesus once said, "I AM the light of the world" (John 9:5), now he says to all of us, "You are the light of the world ... Arise, shine, for your light has come, and the glory of the Lord rises upon you" (Matthew 5:14 with Isaiah 60:1). We are to be salt for the world and light for the world – to the glory of God!

Prayer

Father, you are indeed worthy and deserving of a people who are fully committed to you and unafraid to say so. Forgive us for sometimes hiding our commitment to you in order to avoid unpleasantness from unbelievers. Help us to be unashamedly salt and light in your world, until you return with the full uncompromising brilliance of your Coming. In Jesus' name, we pray. Amen.

Excursus 2: The Religion of the Pharisees

If we are to understand the Sermon on the Mount, we need to understand who the Pharisees are, since Jesus' exposition of what his Kingdom is like is contrasted with the dominant form of Judaism prevalent in Palestine in Jesus' time, as exemplified in the Pharisees.

Who Were the Pharisees?

The Pharisees were a strict religious sect within Judaism that functioned as a political interest group seeking to reform society by bringing about a strict adherence to the Law, especially as it related to ritual purity.

The name "Pharisee" is apparently derived from the Hebrew word *perusim*, meaning "the separated ones" or "separatists." The term "Pharisee," however, was what those outside the sect called them. The Pharisees themselves apparently didn't have a name for their movement. Rather they considered them-

James J. Tissot, "The Pharisee and the Publican" (1886-96), watercolor, Brooklyn Museum, New York.

selves the true Israel, and referred to themselves as "sages" (*hakamim*). After the destruction of the temple, they used the title "rabbi" for sages.

The Pharisees, as a whole, were not the ruling class, though they sought to influence the ruling class. Nor were they of the priestly class, who tended to conform to the teachings of another religious sect, the Sadducees. Nor were they professional scholars like the "scribes" or "teachers of the law" (though some of these professional scholars identified themselves as Pharisees). The Pharisees were part of a voluntary lay movement that sought to bring a renewed understanding and enforcement of ritual purity in Palestine.

Historical Origins

F.F. Bruce traces the Pharisees to the Hasidim, the "godly people," groups of pious Jews after the exile, who began to meet for mutual encouragement. They deplored the inroads of the Hellenistic way of life into Judaism, and many supported the Hasmoneans and Maccabees in resisting the Greek oppressors and restoring the Temple to the pure worship of Israel's God. Later they broke with John Hyrcanus (which may be one explanation of the name Pharisees, "separatists").

The Pharisees were passionately devoted to the Torah. In the course of their study and application of the law they built up a body of traditional interpretation and application of the law known as "the tradition of the elders." Later generations of rabbis eventually wrote it down about the Second Century AD in what is called the Mishnah, consisting of sixty-two tractates or sections. Later yet, from 400 to 600 AD, a Talmud, or commentary upon and expansion of the Mishnah was developed. These are the basis of the Rabbinical writings that form the literature of present-day Judaism.

Work on the Sabbath

Law: Refrain from work on the Sabbath (Exodus 20:8-11)

Tradition of the Elders: Harvesting is work. Plucking a handful of grain is harvesting. Therefore Jesus' disciples were guilty of breaking the Sabbath by eating some grain plucked in the fields as they passed through (Matthew 12:1-2). Healing is the work a physician performs. Therefore one cannot heal on the Sabbath (Matthew 12:10).

Fasting

Law: Fasting, on special occasions, as a sign of repentance.

Tradition of the Elders: Fast twice a week (Luke 18:12)

Tithe

Law: Tithe, that is, give one tenth, of your income to the Lord (Malachi 3:8-10).

Tradition of the Elders: Tithe everything, even down to garden herbs (Matthew 23:23). Jesus does not reprove them for this.

Washing Hands

Law: Priests are to wash their hands in the Laver before offering sacrifice (Exodus 30:17-21).

Tradition of the Elders: All people are to wash hands before eating lest they pass ritual uncleanness to food, which, when eaten, would render the whole body unclean. Not as a hygienic precaution, but a ritual act of pouring water over the hands up to the wrists (Matthew 15:2).

Honoring Parents

Law: Honor your father and your mother (Exodus 20:12)

Tradition of the Elders: Money may be dedicated to God, which relieves a son from the responsibility of using that money to support one's parents in their old age (Matthew 15:4-6).

Vowing

Law: When a person makes a vow, swearing in the name of the LORD to perform some act, he must keep his vow (Exodus 20:7; Numbers 30:2).

Tradition of the Elders: The Pharisees had developed a deceptive method of swearing. If one swore by the temple, the vow meant nothing, but if one swore by the gold in the temple, then one was obligated to keep one's vow (Matthew 23:16).

The Pharisees' present-day descendents are to be found among the Hassidim, what we refer to in America as the Orthodox branch of Judaism. The men are distinguished by their three-quarter length topcoats, white shirts, and wide-brim black hats (and sometimes ear locks), the traditional clothing their ancestors wore in the Jewish ghettos of European cities.

The Tradition of the Elders

Since the Pharisees were passionate in their desire to obey God's law, they had developed over time an oral tradition, "the tradition of the elders," that put a "hedge" or fence around the Biblical commandments. The idea was that obedience to the tradition of the elders formed a barrier that would prevent a pious Jew from breaking a Biblical commandment itself.

Here's an example, though it didn't seem to be an issue in Jesus' day, but much later. Exodus 23:19 prohibits cooking a kid in its mother's milk. A "hedge" around this law eventually because the requirement to keep a "Kosher kitchen," maintaining two separate sets of cooking utensils, one for dairy products and the other for non-dairy cooking – lest one might inadvertently get some minute portion of milk in a pot that was cooking the meat of a young goat.

Over time, this "tradition of the elders" became a law unto itself, and it is with this oral tradition that we find Jesus clashing. Here are some examples of how this "tradition of the elders" in Jesus' day sometimes conflicted with the true Law in the Word of God.

It must be said in their favor, that the Pharisees were not lukewarm about their faith, but zealous – though sometimes misdirected. The Apostle Paul was raised as a strict Pharisee (Acts 26:5), and sought to purify Judaism by rooting out what he perceived to be the Christian heresy.[1]

Jesus' Criticism of the Pharisees

Jesus faulted the Pharisees at two points in particular.

1. They placed a heavy burden or yoke of law upon the people that God never intended (Matthew 23:4 in contrast with 11:29-30)

2. Many were hypocrites, in that they were much more concerned with the outward appearance of piety and righteousness than with having a pure heart towards God (Matthew 23:5ff and 23:25-28).

Jesus also agreed with them on a number of points. We'll examine some other teachings of the Pharisees later in our study.

---

[1] F.F. Bruce, *New Testament History* (Anchor Books, 1969, reprinted 1972), pp. 67-81. Other resources include: Joachim Jeremias, *Jerusalem in the Time of Jesus* (Fortress Press, 1969, reprinted 1975), pp. 246-267. George Foot Moore, *Judaism in the First Centuries of the Christian Era: The Age of Tannaim* (Hendrickson, 1927, reprinted 1997), 1:56-71. Anthony J. Saldarini, "Pharisees," in *Anchor Bible Dictionary* (Doubleday, 1992), 5:289-303. Stephen Westerholm, "Pharisees," DJG, pp. 609-614. Robert J. Wyatt, "Pharisees," ISBE, 3:822-829.

II. The Kingdom and the Spirit of the Law (5:17-48)

This section of the Sermon on the Mount consists of Jesus' reinterpretation of the Law to bring out the spirit that God intended originally. We'll consider it in six chapters.

3. Fulfillment of the Law (5:17-20)

4. The Spirit of Reconciliation (5:21-26)

5. Adultery, Lust, and the Spirit of Marriage (5:27-30)

6. The Spirit of Marriage. Jesus' Teaching on Divorce (5:27-32 with Matthew 19:1-12)

7. The Spirit of Promising (5:33-37)

8. The Spirit of Love versus Retaliation (5:38-48)

Cosimo Rosselli, detail from "Sermon on the Mount" (1481-82), Fresco, 349 x 570 cm, Sistine Chapel, Vatican.

3. The Spirit of the Law and Reconciliation (5:17-26)

How does the New Testament relate to the Old? How do Spirit-filled Christians relate to the Old Testament saints?

Old versus New, Law versus Grace

Many Christians are quick to throw out the Old Testament. "The God of the Old Testament," they say, "is an angry, vengeful God. So different from Jesus." Most Christians today are unfamiliar with the Old Testament. If anything, they bring only a New Testament to church, and act like the Old Testament no longer has any authority.

Others define it in terms of Law versus Grace, following St. Paul's lead. "I am not under the Old Testament law," they say. "I'm now under the grace of God." True, but just what does that mean?

James J. Tissot, "Jesus Teaching in the Synagogue" (1886-1896), watercolor, Brooklyn Museum, New York.

What did Jesus intend to accomplish? Did Jesus come to do away with the Old Testament?

This very question is at the heart of Jesus' controversy with the Pharisees. (See Excursus 2, "Introduction to the Religion of the Pharisees," above). Jesus doesn't seem concerned to follow the meticulous legal observance of the Pharisees. He heals on the Sabbath. His disciples nibble at grain plucked on the Sabbath. They don't even wash their hands in the prescribed manner! What kind of religion is Jesus propagating? Doesn't he care about the Law?

Not to Abolish but to Fulfill (5:17)

Jesus states his position very clearly:

"Do not think that I have come to abolish the Law or the Prophets; I have not come to abolish them but to fulfill them." (5:17)

What did he mean? First we need to define some of the phrases he uses.

"The Law" refers especially the Torah or Pentateuch, the first five books of the Bible. "The Prophets" include both the writings of the Prophets (what we call the major and minor prophets) as well as Samuel, Kings, and Chronicles (what we call the historical books). Jesus' phrase "The Law and the Prophets" refers to the whole of the Old Testament Scripture.

He contrasts two words: "abolish" and "fulfill."

The word translated "abolish" (NIV) or "destroy" (KJV) is Greek *kataluō*, which means, "destroy, demolish, dismantle," here, ""to end the effect of something" so that it is no longer in force, "do away with, abolish, annul, make invalid, repeal."[1] This is a strong word, used, for example, of the destruction of the temple in Matthew 24:2; 26:61; 27:40. So with it Jesus emphatically denies coming to destroy the law.

Rather he has a very positive view of the law. He speaks in verse 17 like he is on a mission: "I have come ...." He has a very deliberate task before him, to fulfill the law and the prophets. The word translated "fulfill" is Greek *plēroō*, which has the basic meaning of "to make full, fill (full)." It can also mean "bring something to completion, finish something already begun." Or "to bring to a designed end, fulfill" a prophecy, an obligation, a promise, a law, a request, a desire, a hope, a duty, a fate, a destiny, etc. Or "to bring to completion an activity in which one has been involved from its beginning, complete, finish."[2] The precise meaning of this common word must be determined by its context.

Certainly Jesus came to make the law itself full. The Pharisees, in their attempt to obey legalistic minutiae had prescribed and limited the application of the law. Jesus wants his followers to see what the law really implies – which is far beyond the Pharisees' safe interpretations. For example, when the law said, "Thou shalt not kill," explains Jesus, it means more than the act of murder, but the anger and lack of respect for a person that motivate the act (5:21-26). Jesus gives the same sort of reinterpretation to popular concepts of adultery (5:27-30), divorce (5:31-32), oath-taking (5:33-37), retaliation (5:38-42), and love for enemies (5:43-48). Helping people to understand the

---

[1] *Kataluō*, BDAG 521-522, 3.a.
[2] *Plēroō*, BDAG 827-828.

full depth and spirit of the law is certainly part of his mission. But, as we'll see in a moment, there was more to his mission of fulfilling the law.

Jots and Tittles (5:18)

First, we need to see how emphatically Jesus spoke these words. He wanted everyone to see how deeply he honored and believed the words of the Law and the Prophets.

He begins with the phrase, "Verily I say unto you ...." It is used as a preface or solemn formula of affirmation to some of Jesus' most definitive statements, and means "truly," and is literally the word "amen." Next he said,

> "Till heaven and earth pass, one jot or one tittle shall in no wise pass from the law, till all be fulfilled." (5:18, KJV)

The NIV translates it:

> "... Until heaven and earth disappear, not the smallest letter, not the least stroke of a pen, will by any means disappear from the Law until everything is accomplished." (5:18)

Just what is a jot or a tittle?

The English word "jot" is Greek *iota*, a letter of the Greek alphabet that corresponds to our letter "i". Evidently it was also the equivalent of the Aramaic and Hebrew letter *yod*, which is written like our apostrophe ('), just a small stroke of the pen.

A "tittle" (rhythms with "little") is Greek *keraia*, and means "literally 'horn,' 'projection, hook' as part of a letter, a 'serif'."[3] You can see how a tiny part of a letter is important when you compare the lower case letter "l" with the number "1". The difference is in merely a "tittle."

The emphasis in these two words is on tiny, small, minute. The NIV captures the sense well: "I tell you the truth, until heaven and earth disappear, not the smallest letter, not the least stroke of a pen, will by any means disappear from the Law until everything is accomplished." In other words, Jesus didn't just come to round out the big themes of the Bible, but to fulfill or accomplish even the tiny prophecies and verses. The sentence is an emphatic one.

Practicing and Teaching (5:19)

But it is followed by an even stronger sentence:

> "Anyone who breaks one of the least of these commandments and teaches others to do the same will be called least in the kingdom of heaven, but whoever practices and teaches these commands will be called great in the kingdom of heaven." (5:19)

---

[3] *Keraia*, BDAG 540.

This should set us on our heels. If we think that we can ignore the teachings of the Old Testament, we'd better think again. Jesus holds us responsible to both practice and teach to our children the commandments of the Lord. We hear a lot of talk about grace, but Jesus speaks pretty clearly here and elsewhere of commandments and obedience. (See, for example, John 14:15; 15:10; 1 John 2:3; 3:22, 24; 5:3.) A disciple's life is one of learning and following his master.

We see this kind of comparison of least and greatest two other times in Matthew:

> "I tell you the truth: Among those born of women there has not risen anyone greater than John the Baptist; yet he who is least in the kingdom of heaven is greater than he." (11:11)

> "Therefore, whoever humbles himself like this child is the greatest in the kingdom of heaven." (18:4)

It doesn't seem that salvation, or entrance into the kingdom, is the issue, but one's standing among the other citizens of the kingdom.

Surpassing the Pharisees' Righteousness (5:20)

Jesus also makes it clear that he isn't talking about a new legalism. The Pharisees were devotees of rigorous law-keeping of the minutiae of the law as it had been passed down to them in an oral tradition called "the tradition of the elders." Tithing herbs from the garden and dribbling water on the tips of one's fingers and allowing it to run down to the wrist were part of this scrupulous observance.

Among the common people, the Pharisees were considered in some ways as the holiest of people. If *they* weren't keeping the law adequately, how could *anyone* keep it? So Jesus' next statement must have shocked his hearers and angered the Pharisees:

> "For I tell you that unless your righteousness surpasses that of the Pharisees and the teachers of the law, you will certainly not enter the kingdom of heaven." (5:20)

How could anyone's righteousness surpass that of the most righteous people in the land? In the remainder of the chapter, Jesus begins to explain how a right observance of the law is not a superficial fulfillment of the exterior, but a living out of the very spirit of the law. And he explains what he means by contrasting with the true spirit of the law what was the popular view of certain commands – murder, adultery, divorce, oath-taking, retaliation, and hating enemies.

How Did Jesus Fulfill the Law?

While our text doesn't spell out the ways that Jesus fulfilled the law, it might be helpful to review them briefly. One way to view the Law is as:

1. The *civil law* that governed the nation Israel,

2. The *religious law* that detailed the sacrifices and temple ceremonies required for the forgiveness of sin, and

3. The *moral law*, such as that found in the Ten Commandments.

1. Civil Law

Jesus fulfilled the civil law that described property rights, civil liability, and inheritance. These were designed to govern Israel as a theocracy, that is, a nation with God as their king. The theocracy of Israel finally passed away when the last king of Judah was deposed and the nation was taken into exile. Never again was Israel an independent nation. When the people returned, they did so as vassals of the Persians, later the Greeks, and still later the Romans. Only for brief periods did Israel exist as an independently governed nation. The Kingdom of God had seemingly come to an end.

But that Kingdom was fulfilled in Jesus himself. (See Excursus 1 above, "What Is the Kingdom of Heaven?") When the Jewish leaders rejected King Jesus, the kingdom was removed from Israel. Jesus said,

> "Therefore I tell you that the kingdom of God will be taken away from you and given to a people who will produce its fruit" (Matthew 21:43).

The Gentiles now had an opportunity to be subjects of the King as the gospel went global.

2. Religious or Ceremonial Law

Exodus and Leviticus describe in great detail the construction of a tabernacle (later, the temple) and the sacrifices required to atone for sin. "Without the shedding of blood there is no forgiveness of sins," we are reminded in Hebrews 9:22b. But the New Testament describes how Jesus, as "the Lamb of God that takes away the sin of the world" (John 1:29), poured out his blood for the forgiveness of sins (Matthew 26:28), once for all and for all time (Hebrews 10:10). The Letter to the Hebrews explains how Jesus is the fulfillment of the Law. So in himself, Jesus fulfilled the religious or ceremonial law.

3. Moral Law

The final kind of law is what we might call the moral law, those moral principles that endure from one age to another. We find them, for example, in the Ten Commandments.

"Thou shalt not kill ... thou shalt not commit adultery ... thou shalt not steal ... thou shalt not bear false witness against your neighbor ...." In the *Shema* we read,

> "Hear, O Israel: The Lord our God, the Lord is one. Love the Lord your God with all your heart and with all your soul and with all your strength" (Deuteronomy 6:4-5).

> "Love your neighbor as yourself" (Leviticus 19:18).

Jesus came to fulfill the Kingdom his Father had established, to fulfill the Law his Father had instituted, and to live out in his life the quality of life to which the Law aspired. "I didn't come to abolish the Law and the Prophets," Jesus said, "but to fulfill them."

Q1. (Matthew 5:17-20) Can you see any tendencies in the church today to effectively "abolish" the Old Testament from our Christian faith? What does a "Christian" legalism look like in a church? What does it look like in a church where there are no moral standards and no obedience expected of Christians?
http://www.joyfulheart.com/forums/index.php?showtopic=739

The Spirit of Reconciliation (5:21-26)

Jesus is perturbed that the Pharisees have so defined the Law in their own terms that they have missed the point. And so he begins to expound the Law as it pertains to six subjects: murder, adultery, divorce, oath-taking, retaliation, and love for one's enemy. Instead of a litany of commandments, Jesus looks to the spirit of the Law.

James J. Tissot, "The Exhortation to the Apostles" (1886-1896), watercolor, Brooklyn Museum, New York.

You have heard that it was said ... but I tell you ...

Each of these subjects begins with an interesting phrase, "You have heard that it was said ... but I tell you ..." (5:21-22, 27-28, 33-34, 38-39, 43-44). Each of these formulas contain the Greek word *errethē* (Aorist Passive of *legō*). This is not the word Jesus uses to quote the Old Testament. It becomes obvious by the time you come to the quotation in 5:43, that he is quoting the oral tradition, the "tradition of the elders," not the scripture directly. (5:43 reads, "You have heard that it was said, 'Love your neighbor' and hate your enemy' ..."). Yes, the Pharisees quoted the Pentateuch, but they went beyond it with their own interpretation, limiting and circumscribing its meaning. Jesus is explaining the actual spirit of the Law, as only God Himself can expound it.

Do Not Murder (5:21)

"You have heard that it was said to the people long ago, 'Do not murder, and anyone who murders will be subject to judgment.'" (5:21)

The Sixth Commandment is "Thou shalt not kill" (KJV, Exodus 20:13). Certainly those who murder will be subject to judgment. The "tradition of the elders" would agree.

Anger and Insult (5:22)

But Jesus goes to the heart of the Law as he expounds the motivation behind murder – anger.

"But I tell you that anyone who is angry with his brother will be subject to judgment. Again, anyone who says to his brother, 'Raca,' is answerable to the Sanhedrin. But anyone who says, 'You fool!' will be in danger of the fire of hell." (5:22)

Let's examine the Greek words used in verses 21-22:

- *Phoneuō* - "murder, kill."[4]
- *Orgizō* - "be angry."[5]
- *Rhaka* - "a term of abuse / put-down relating to lack of intelligence, numskull, fool (in effect verbal bullying)," derived from the Aramaic word meaning "empty one," found in the Talmud, "empty-head."[6]
- *Mōros* - "foolish, stupid,"[7] from which we get our word "moron."

---

[4] *Phoneuō*, BDAG 1063.
[5] *Orgizō*, BDAG 721.
[6] *Rhaka*, BDAG 903.
[7] *Mōros*, BDAG 663.

- *Synedrion* - "a governing board, council," then "the high council in Jerusalem, Sanhedrin."[8]
- *Gehenna* - Gehenna, "'Valley of the Sons of Hinnom,' a ravine south of Jerusalem. There, according to later Jewish popular belief, God's final judgment was to take place. In the gospels it is the place of punishment in the next life, 'hell.'"[9]

A.B. Bruce distinguishes between the word "Raca" and "fool" in this way: "*Raca* expresses contempt for a man's head – you stupid! [The Greek word] *mōre* expresses contempt for his heart and character – you scoundrel!"[10]

This ought to scare us. Who hasn't been angry and insulted someone? Of course, we can get legalistic and say that we haven't used the exact word "Raca" or "fool." But that is the same kind of word gymnastics for which Jesus condemned the Pharisees. Jesus is saying that we are guilty before God for a heart that lashes out in anger and venom. Whether or not a person's life is terminated as a result is not the point.

When I was a boy, we would parrot this saying to someone who called us a name:

> "Sticks and stones may break my bones,
> but words can never hurt me."

Unfortunately, this children's chant is false. Words *do* hurt. Names injure us – sometimes for life. How many of you or your friends have spent years struggling with what your father or mother said to you – plagued by it, your self-confidence destroyed. Anger, and the vile venom it inspires, kill the spirit. And those who spew this acid on those about them are not free from judgment. The God who condemns murder also condemns angry insult, for they both come from the same root.

Q2. (Matthew 5:21-22) Why does Jesus treat calling someone a fool in the same classification as murder? Does this mean that murder is no worse than an angry insult in God's eyes? How would we act differently if we actually *believed* that angry attitudes towards others are viewed by God as murder?
http://www.joyfulheart.com/forums/index.php?showtopic=740

Woe to You Hypocrites!

Man looks on the exterior, the action, but God examines the heart. And in the heart is

[8] *Synedrion*, BDAG 967.
[9] *Gehenna*, BDAG 190-191.
[10] A.B. Bruce, Commentary on the Synoptic Gospels in *The Expositor's Greek Testament* (1897), p. 107.

the root of murder. Legalism is an exterior thing, but the life of a follower of Jesus begins in the heart.

> "Woe to you, teachers of the law and Pharisees, you hypocrites! You clean the *outside* of the cup and dish, but *inside* they are full of greed and self-indulgence. Blind Pharisee! First clean the inside of the cup and dish, and then the outside also will be clean.
>
> Woe to you, teachers of the law and Pharisees, you hypocrites! You are like white-washed tombs, which look beautiful on the *outside* but on the *inside* are full of dead men's bones and everything unclean. In the same way, on the *outside* you appear to people as righteous but on the *inside* you are full of hypocrisy and wickedness." (Matthew 23:25-28)

No, Jesus didn't come to abolish the law, but to bring out its fullness, to fulfill it.

The Fire of Hell (22c)

So what of the upstanding moral people who never kill, who drive the speed limit, who never break the law? What of them? Are *they* to be consigned to the fires of hell for hatred in their hearts? (See Excursus 3 below, "Did Jesus Believe in Hell?") The answer we must come to is: Yes!

Sometimes we labor under the ancient myth that we can earn heaven by our good deeds. No, Jesus would say, we must repent! Jesus taught,

> "But the things that come out of the mouth come from the heart, and these make a man 'unclean.' For out of the heart come evil thoughts, murder, adultery, sexual immorality, theft, false testimony, slander. These are what make a man 'unclean'; but eating with unwashed hands does not make him 'unclean'" (Matthew 15:18-20).

The argument in the passage just quoted was part of Jesus' running discussion with the Pharisees about externals versus internals. And with us, too, Jesus carries on this continuing discussion. Cleanse the heart, and then the exterior actions will follow.

The Cleansing Process

So often when someone from a rough lifestyle becomes a Christian, we church people are quick to get him to conform to our standards of speech, dress, and morals. But you don't learn how to "walk the walk" from learning to "talk the talk." That's backwards. It is the Holy Spirit of God that cleanses us, and he works from the inside out, in an ever-broadening cycle – conviction, repentance, and change; conviction, repentance, and change. Don't feel you have to do God's cleansing work for him when someone becomes a Christian. Love them. Support them. Pray for them. You expect to change a few diapers with a newborn. "God catches his fish before he cleans them."

Can we live so circumspectly that we do not break the law of the pure heart? Can we live in such a way that we need no forgiveness? No. "The heart is deceitful above all things, and desperately corrupt; who can understand it?" (RSV, Jeremiah 17:9). Why did Jesus die on the cross? Because there was no other way to atone for our sins. "This is my blood of the new covenant, which is poured out for many for the forgiveness of sins," said Jesus (Matthew 26:28). The Law, the Apostle Paul observes, is not intended to bring salvation but "that through the commandment sin might become utterly sinful" (Romans 7:13).

So if we are frightened by Jesus' stern condemnation of anger and insult and we see the flickering flames of hell licking at us for our heart wickedness, then we've gotten the point that Jesus intended. "Repent, for the kingdom of heaven is near," was Jesus' message (Matthew 4:17) and that of his cousin John the Baptist (Matthew 3:2). People flocked to them and were baptized, washing away their sins, because they became aware of their heart wickedness and need for cleansing.

> "All the people, even the tax collectors, when they heard Jesus' words, acknowledged that God's way was right, because they had been baptized by John. But the Pharisees and experts in the law rejected God's purpose for themselves, because they had not been baptized by John" (Luke 7:29-30).

Which is your heart most like? A repentant tax collector or a self-justifying Pharisee?

First, go be reconciled to your brother (5:23-24)

> 23 "Therefore, if you are offering your gift at the altar and there remember that your brother has something against you, 24 leave your gift there in front of the altar. First go and be reconciled to your brother; then come and offer your gift." (5:23-24)

So if anger, murder, and insult are condemned by the Law as expounded by Jesus, what is *approved* by the law? What is the *positive command* we are to fulfill? "Be reconciled to your brother" (5:24).

How do we fulfill this law? If we are worshipping and remember that our brother has something against us, we are to leave our gift behind and first be reconciled to our brother. After we have done that, we can come back and resume our worship.

Does this sound a bit radical to your ears? It sounded radical to First Century ears, as well. Jesus sometimes rammed home his points through hyperbole, over-statement, so they would be unforgettable. Is this hyperbole? Perhaps.

But Jesus' clear point is that worship – seeking to honor God by bringing an offering – is a mockery if we don't first repent of our sins and carry out that repentance to its logical conclusion. That point isn't radical. It is taught throughout the Scripture in such passages as:

"Does the Lord delight in burnt offerings and sacrifices
as much as in obeying the voice of the Lord?
To obey is better than sacrifice,
and to heed is better than the fat of rams" (1 Samuel 15:22).

"Rend your heart and not your garments. Return to the Lord your God..." (Joel 2:13).

"You do not delight in sacrifice, or I would bring it;
you do not take pleasure in burnt offerings.
The sacrifices of God are a broken spirit;
a broken and contrite heart,
O God, you will not despise" (Psalm 51:16-17).

Is Reconciliation Always Possible?

We need to say, however, that Jesus' words, "First, go and be reconciled to your brother," imply that you have offended your brother and need to make amends. There may well be estrangement that we have little to do with and cannot change. The willingness to reconcile must be shared by the other party. Don't beat yourself up over this. But make sure that you have made right what you need to, and that your anger and insult and self-righteousness about it have been replaced by humility and a willingness to reconcile.

Sometimes we have hurt someone deeply and it is fully our fault, but when we go to humble ourselves and seek forgiveness we are snubbed. We may be snubbed, but we must still go and seek reconciliation.

Lest we think we are in the clear about this, be aware that elsewhere Jesus spoke about another aspect of reconciliation – our willingness to forgive those who have offended us.

"And when you stand praying, if you hold anything against anyone, forgive him, so that your Father in heaven may forgive you your sins." (Mark 11:25)

Reconciliation may be possible if we will humble ourselves. And even if it is not possible, we must make a sincere attempt if we would seek to fulfill the spirit of the Law. After all, the Law is not really about murder and stealing. It is about love and reconciliation. *That* is the spirit of the Law.

Q3. (Matthew 5:23-24) What's wrong with worshipping while a brother has something against us (or us against a brother, Mark 11:25)? What is the appropriate action for us to take? How far should we go to bring about reconciliation with someone whom we have offended? Are there any situations that we shouldn't try to resolve? Or that we can't resolve?

http://www.joyfulheart.com/forums/index.php?showtopic=741

Settle matters quickly with your accuser (5:25-26)

Jesus concludes this teaching on reconciliation with an example from a mini-parable.

"Settle matters quickly with your adversary who is taking you to court. Do it while you are still with him on the way, or he may hand you over to the judge, and the judge may hand you over to the officer, and you may be thrown into prison. I tell you the truth, you will not get out until you have paid the last penny" (5:25-26)

The parable assumes that you owe your accuser a debt of some kind, and to collect on it he is taking you to small claims court. Jesus is saying: Don't wait until you get to court to work out some kind of deal; settle out of court. Because if the court has to decide the matter, you will be thrown into debtor's prison and won't get out until every last cent is paid.

We don't have debtor's prisons today, but they were common in Western jurisprudence until recently. On the surface they seem stupid: If a person is in prison he can't work to repay his debt. But what happened when you are thrown into debtor's prison, was that your family and friends would come up with the money in order to get you out. Then you have to live the rest of your life with your family glowering at you, and never letting you forget the hardship you have caused them.

So in this mini-parable, Jesus is saying, settle quickly, before you get to court. Settle quickly or you'll be stuck for every last cent that is due.

What is the point of the parable in this context? Jesus is teaching his hearers to reconcile quickly with those they have wronged and not to put it off. The implication is that if they wait for God to settle the matter at his bar of justice, that judgment will exacting and harsh punishment.

You remember that this teaching on murder began with the concepts of accountability and justice: "... subject to judgment ... answerable to the Council ... in danger of the fire of hell." Jesus' mini-parable is only a thinly-veiled picture of us having to stand before God for every one of our sins unless we repent now.

Q4. (Matthew 5:25-26) What is the point of Jesus' parable of settling out of court? Who are we supposed to settle with, according to this parable? What does "settling" entail? What are the reasons that we should settle?

http://www.joyfulheart.com/forums/index.php?showtopic=742

The Golden Center

In a sense, the Law "Thou shalt not kill" is an outpost to regulate the limits of our behavior, but the Golden Center is something else. Is God seeking non-murderers? No. He is seeking those who do not let anger and hatred live in their hearts at all. He is seeking those who will show mercy, those who will forgive, those who will, in a word, love.

Jesus came to fulfill the Law and the Prophets, not to abolish them. One day an expert in the Law asked Jesus this question:

"Teacher, which is the greatest commandment in the Law?"

Jesus replied: " 'Love the Lord your God with all your heart and with all your soul and with all your mind.' This is the first and greatest commandment. And the second is like it: 'Love your neighbor as yourself.' All the Law and the Prophets hang on these two commandments" (Matthew 22:36-40).

And so what seemed complex to the legalists becomes much simpler to grasp. "Love your neighbor as yourself." That is the aim of the whole law, straight from the mouth of God himself in the Person of Jesus Christ.

Q5. (Matthew 5:21-26) Verses 21-22 are about murder, anger, and insult. Verses 23-24 discuss some fault against one's brother. Verses 25-26 discuss settling a civil suit before going to court. What is the overarching theme of Jesus' teaching in our entire passage, verses 21-26?

http://www.joyfulheart.com/forums/index.php?showtopic=743

Prayer

Father, when you examine our hearts and our attitudes, we are sinners. No, we aren't literal murderers, but you couldn't tell that from our hearts. Forgive us. Cleanse us. And infuse us with the kind of love you have that can love and redeem us in all our conflicted rebellion. Transform us by your Spirit, we pray, in Jesus' name. Amen.

Excursus 3: Did Jesus Believe in Hell?

If you were to listen to the popular mind about hell, you'd think that it was an invention of the church to keep people in line. That the religion of Jesus is much too loving and forgiving to send people to hell. The facts are different. Jesus says more about hell and eternal punishment than anyone else in the entire Bible. The teaching comes from his own lips and we must take it with utmost seriousness.

Some word confusion tends to cloud the issue. There are two Greek words that are translated by "hell" in the King James Version. Here are the definitions:

Hades

The first Greek word is *Hadēs*, "(originally a proper noun, god of the underworld), then the nether world, Hades as place of the dead."[1]. Here are the occurrences of the word *Hades* in the Gospels:

> "And you, Capernaum, will you be lifted up to the skies? No, you will go down to the depths (*Hadēs*). If the miracles that were performed in you had been performed in Sodom, it would have remained to this day" (Matthew 11:23; similarly Luke 10:15).

> "And I tell you that you are Peter, and on this rock I will build my church, and the gates of Hades will not overcome it" (Matthew 16:18).

> "In hell (*Hadēs*), where he was in torment, [the rich man] looked up and saw Abraham far away, with Lazarus by his side. So he called to him, 'Father Abraham, have pity on me and send Lazarus to dip the tip of his finger in water and cool my tongue, because I am in agony in this fire' " (Luke 16:23-24)

Hieronymus Bosch (Dutch painter, c. 1450-1516), "Hell" (after 1490), Palazzo Ducale, Venice.

Gehenna

The other Greek word is *gehenna*, Gehenna, "'Valley of the Sons of Hinnom,' a ravine

[1] *Hadēs*, BDAG 19.

south of Jerusalem. There, according to later Jewish popular belief, God's final judgment was to take place. In the gospels it is the place of punishment in the next life, 'hell.'"[2] Here are the references to Gehenna in the gospels:

> "But I tell you that anyone who is angry with his brother will be subject to judgment. Again, anyone who says to his brother, 'Raca,' is answerable to the Sanhedrin. But anyone who says, 'You fool!' will be in danger of the fire of hell (*Gehenna*)." (Matthew 5:22)

> "If your right eye causes you to sin, gouge it out and throw it away. It is better for you to lose one part of your body than for your whole body to be thrown into hell (*Gehenna*). And if your right hand causes you to sin, cut it off and throw it away. It is better for you to lose one part of your body than for your whole body to go into hell (*Gehenna*)." (Matthew 5:29-30. Similarly 18:9 which uses the phrase "fire of hell")

> In the parallel passage, Mark's gospel spells it out further: "... hell (*Gehenna*), where the fire never goes out." (Mark 9:43, 45, 47)

> "Do not be afraid of those who kill the body but cannot kill the soul. Rather, be afraid of the One who can destroy both soul and body in hell (*Gehenna*)." (Matthew 10:28; similarly Luke 12:5)

> "Woe to you, teachers of the law and Pharisees, you hypocrites! You travel over land and sea to win a single convert, and when he becomes one, you make him twice as much a son of hell (*Gehenna*) as you are." (Matthew 23:15)

> "You snakes! You brood of vipers! How will you escape being condemned to hell (*Gehenna*)?" (Matthew 23:33)

Of course, in this short article I haven't analyzed Jesus' use of *Hades* and *Gehenna*. But I think that even a cursory reading of the gospels indicates that Jesus believed in the existence of hell as a place of fiery torment for those who had sinned.

---

[2] *Gehenna*, BDAG 190-191.

4. Adultery, Lust, and the Spirit of Marriage (5:27-30)

In the short scope of the Sermon on the Mount, Jesus could only cover the most important of subjects. One which he selected was adultery. In our day adultery is rampant. Some estimate that half of husbands commit adultery sometime in their marriage, along with a

Théodore Chassériau (French painter, 1819-1856), detail from "Susanna and the Elders" (1856), Louvre, Paris. The famous story is from the apocryphal chapter 13 of Daniel, where lecherous elders try to blackmail a virtuous wife whom they are ogling.

third of wives. But the problem begins, Jesus teaches us, in the heart.

Legalistic Righteousness

The Pharisees felt secure in observing the Seventh Commandment (Exodus 20:14), and Jesus states their sentiment:

"You have heard that it was said, 'Do not commit adultery.'" (5:27)

In our day this attitude is expressed in a wife's careless permission, "I don't care how much you look, just don't touch."

Lust in the Heart

However, Jesus goes beyond the letter to the spirit of the law: "But I tell you that anyone who looks at a woman lustfully has already committed adultery with her in his heart" (5:28). Is that really what the Law had in mind, you wonder? Yes, indeed. The Tenth Commandment is pretty specific:

"You shall not covet your neighbor's house. You shall not covet your neighbor's wife, or his manservant or maidservant, his ox or donkey, or anything that belongs to your neighbor" (Exodus 20:17).

The Old Testament word translated "covet" is Hebrew *ḥāmad*, which has a basic meaning: "desire, delight in." However, it is often used negatively, as here, with the meaning:"inordinate, ungoverned selfish desire," sometimes of "lustful desire."[1]

Q1. (Matthew 5:27-30; Exodus 20:17) What is the point of similarity between adultery and lust? What is the difference? How does lust break the Tenth Commandment? http://www.joyfulheart.com/forums/index.php?showtopic=744

The heart of man is the problem according to Jesus. Lust is a thing of the heart. He teaches:

> "For out of the heart come evil thoughts, murder, adultery, sexual immorality, theft, false testimony, slander." (Matthew 15:19)

Indeed, he echoes the words of the prophet Jeremiah:

> "The heart is deceitful above all things, and desperately wicked: who can know it?" (KJV, Jeremiah 17:9)

If the woman isn't married and the man isn't married, and they lust for one another, is it still wrong? Technically, it can't be adultery if neither is married. Here we are dealing with technicalities again. The self-righteous Pharisees were the fathers of such technicalities. But Jesus also uses the Greek word *porneia* (Matthew 15:19; Mark 7:21), translated "fornications" (KJV) or "sexual immorality" (NIV), that is, "unlawful sexual intercourse, prostitution, unchastity, fornication," applied in the New Testament to all kinds of illicit sexual conduct inside and outside of marriage.[2] We can't get off that easily.

Natural Sexual Desire versus Lust

Is there any hope for a man? From the first stirrings of adolescence, hormones begin to surge through boys turning them into men. Sex is one of the strongest drives we have. Is this natural sexual desire wrong?

No, natural desire for the opposite sex is normal and necessary. Men desire women and vice versa, families are formed, children produced. That is what God intended.

Like any good gift, however, Satan is quick to pervert or twist it into something God didn't intend. Food is good, but it can lead to ill health when eaten in overabundance. Wine is God's good gift, but can cause drunkenness when taken to excess. Money is good, but can corrupt the soul when worshipped. And so on.

[1] *Hāmad*, BDB 326, TWOT 295.
[2] *Porneia*, BDAG 854, 1.

Now, I've heard some argue that man is an animal, and thus a desire to mate with any and every female is entirely natural and should not be censured. Common sense tells us, however, that unrestrained sex leads to broken families, fatherless children, and general chaos. If unrestrained sex were man's destiny, why should it turn out so badly for all concerned?

We don't see that view in God's Word. We read in Genesis 2 about a man and a woman.

> "For this reason a man will leave his father and mother and be united to his wife [literally, "woman"], and they will become one flesh." (Genesis 2:24)

This unity of husband and wife is the basic unit. Society has sometimes allowed polygamy (and in those societies God allowed men of faith to have more than one wife, e.g. Jacob and David). But when we examine the family life of these polygamous unions, we see envy, strife, and competition rather than peace. In the New Testament, leaders of the church are to reflect the ancient and holy ideal that God instituted in the Garden:

> "Now the overseer must be above reproach, the husband of but one wife...." (1 Timothy 3:2; see also Titus 1:6; 1 Timothy 5:9)

The sex drive is a good thing, but only good when it is exercised within the boundaries God has set, namely, marriage. Outside of marriage, sex may "feel so right" but bring a harvest of bad fruit. Inside of marriage it bonds husbands to wives and wives to husbands, and, God willing, children that can grow up within a stable family environment.

Q2. God purposely created us with a good and natural sexual desire. How do we distinguish between that God-given sexual desire and forbidden lust?
http://www.joyfulheart.com/forums/index.php?showtopic=745

Pornography, the "Victimless" Crime

Along with the "free sex" movement that began in the 1960s came a loosening of restrictions on pornography. If "looking on a woman to commit adultery with her in your heart" is Jesus' definition of the spirit of adultery, then pornography fits the description precisely, defined as: "the depiction of erotic behavior (as in pictures or writing) intended to cause sexual excitement."[3]

---

[3] *Merriam-Webster's 11th Collegiate Dictionary* (2003).

Where pornography was once available only in sleazy porn shops, today it has become common in our society, abundant in libraries, bookshops, and video stores – now piped into homes on the Internet and cable television.

There are no victims here, argue the pornographers and their allies. An increasing body of evidence disagrees. While a portion of the feminist movement supports pornography as a free speech issue, a significant slice opposes pornography as degrading and dangerous to women. Here are some of the arguments against pornography:

1. Pornography helps men view women as mere sex objects.

2. Pornography lowers moral values in individuals and society resulting in the acceptability and/or legalization of prostitution, fornication, adultery, and other sexual perversions.

3. Pornography creates unrealistic expectations of sex and sexual practices that spouses may be unable or unwilling to fulfill.

4. Pornography isolates sexual fulfillment from a caring relationship with another human being, rendering it essentially selfish.

5. Pornography exploits young women's naiveté and need for money, prostituting images of their bodies to fulfill men's lusts.

6. Pornography is linked to crimes of rape, incest, and sexual abuse of children.

7. The pornographic industry is increasingly controlled by organized crime.

8. Pornography can become psychologically addictive, leading many men to crave more and more bizarre sexual fantasies to stimulate them.

As our society embraces pornography as a harmless outlet, it can't help but increase problems of individuals and society as a whole.

Who are the "victims" whom Satan deceives and pollutes through pornography?

*   The women who pose.

*   The men who view and become addicted despite their shame.

*   The wives who suffer isolation, shame, and assault.

*   The children who are abused.

*   The women who are raped.

*   The society that bears the cumulative pain of divorce, crime, and disorder.

Victims? We all are victims.

Q3. (Matthew 5:28) What is wrong with pornography? What is wrong with going to prostitutes? Who are the victims of this "victimless" activity?
http://www.joyfulheart.com/forums/index.php?showtopic=746

Cutting off Your Hand – or Worse (5:29-30)

> "If your right eye causes you to sin, gouge it out and throw it away. It is better for you to lose one part of your body than for your whole body to be thrown into hell. And if your right hand causes you to sin, cut it off and throw it away. It is better for you to lose one part of your body than for your whole body to go into hell" (5:29-30).

So what are we to do when we find ourselves looking at women wrongly? Grasp an eyeball and yank it out of its socket? Is that what Jesus intended? Back in the early years of Christianity, an influential Alexandrian Christian teacher, Origin (187-254 AD), was so plagued by sexual temptations that he castrated himself. Is self-mutilation Jesus' intent?

I don't think so. Jesus, like all of us, sometimes uses hyperbole – overstatement – to make a point. When Jesus speaks of a camel going through the eye of a needle (Matthew 19:24), for example, it was hyperbole, an indication of impossibility. When he says a man should hate his father and mother, wife and children (Luke 14:26), he is employing hyperbole. When we say, "I'll swear on a stack of Bibles," or "I wouldn't do that in a million years," we are using hyperbole to make a point.

When Jesus speaks about cutting off a hand or gouging out an eye, he is speaking in hyperbole. If we were intended to take it literally, we should expect to find other examples in the Word as the apostles sought to expound on and teach it. We don't find anything of the sort. The closest is Paul's statement, "I beat my body and make it my slave" (1 Corinthians 9:27).

While Origin's heart may have been right, he misinterpreted Jesus' words. Saints and hermits throughout the ages have discovered that while you can blind yourself or isolate yourself from women, you cannot isolate yourself from your own mind and heart.

Jesus' words meant to convey to us that we are to take sexual lust with utmost seriousness. He intended us to understand that lust can lead us down the road to hell itself. (See Excursus 3 above: "Did Jesus Believe in Hell?")

Jesus said:

> "But I tell you that anyone who looks at a woman lustfully has already committed adultery with her in his heart." (Matthew 5:28)

Therefore, he is saying, unless you and I want to stand as guilty before God as one who commits physical adultery, we must repent rather than excuse ourselves.

Rather than pass off lust as a common denominator of males, Jesus intended that we flee from lust with as much determination as we flee from adultery or fornication (1 Corinthians 6:18). Make no mistake, lust can damn us. We must repent or be damned – or try to explain away Jesus' own words in 5:30.

Breaking Free from Lust and Lure

So if you have been captured by a habit of lust or pornography, how do you break free? It is difficult. If you have practiced a habit over a period of years, you will not break it in a moment. It will take determination and a healthy dose of God's grace to cleanse you when you fail. But it *is* possible to break free from lust. Here are some steps that can help.

1. Call an attraction to pornography what it is – adultery of the heart – a spiritual addiction.
2. Understand something of the nature of the addiction. For example, what is the "love hunger" that pornography feeds and what are the "triggers" that result in viewing of pornography?4
3. Come to a firm conviction that lust is wrong. Deal with each of the rationalizations you have made for your sin. Write them down to look at when you are tempted.
4. Stop feeding your lust. Get rid of anything in your home that triggers this lust.
    *   Throw out any pornographic materials you possess.
    *   Until you get victory over this it may involve cutting off the cable capability that pipes pornography into your home.
    *   Ask the phone company block all 900 number calls.
    *   Purchase a service that filters out pornography from your computers – not just for your children's sake, but for your sake as well.
5. Share with someone close to you your struggle with this sin and become accountable to this person.[5]

---

[4] You may find some help from Dennis Rupert's "Weapons for the War against Lust and Sexual Immorality" (www.new-life.net).

[5] Covenant Eyes (www.covenanteyes.com) is software that e-mails a report of Internet sites you view to the

- Ask for this person's prayer support and confess your sins to him (James 5:16).
- Seek counsel for your problem from a pastor or Christian counselor.

6. Use the weapons of prayer, scripture reading, and fasting.

7. Accept God's grace and complete forgiveness toward you as his child, even if you fall and sin again. The woman taken in adultery didn't hear condemnation from Jesus, but love and encouragement: "Neither do I condemn you. Go, and sin no more" (John 8:11).

Q4. (Matthew 5:28) Sex is very closely tied to our core sense of person. This means that as we are healed in our view towards sex, it goes a long way toward making us whole inside. How would you counsel a brother who shared with you that he had trouble with pornography? How can you protect yourself against temptation over the Internet? At the beach or poolside? With your TV?

http://www.joyfulheart.com/forums/index.php?showtopic=747

Looking with Love

God wants us to be able to look on members of the opposite sex with love rather than lust. If we are struggling with homosexual lust, he wants us to be able to look on the members of our own sex with a pure love and without lust. This is his plan. (See below Excursus 4. Homosexual Lust.)

But the war against lust is not essentially a negative one, a defensive battle. If lust and adultery are the negatives, what is the positive? If the law tells us what *not* to do; what does it direct us to practice? "Teacher," Jesus' enemies asked him to trick him, "which is the greatest commandment in the Law?" Jesus replied:

> "'**Love the Lord your God** with all your heart and with all your soul and with all your mind.' This is the first and greatest commandment. And the second is like it: '**Love your neighbor** as yourself.' All the Law and the Prophets hang on these two commandments." (Matthew 22:36-40)

Jesus calls us to look with love. Men in a church are to:

> "Treat ... younger women as sisters, with absolute purity." (1 Timothy 5:2).

The reason brothers don't usually lust for their sisters – beyond a strong cultural

---

accountability partner of your choice.

incest taboo – is because they care for them as people. Their relationship goes beyond the physical exterior to the real person who has longings and disappointments, a girl with potential and hope and pain. We love our sisters as people. That is what it is all about.

Job said,

"I made a covenant with my eyes not to look lustfully at a girl." (Job 31:1)

How then can I look at her? As a sister. As a wonderful and fragile human being. As a person whom God loves. If I can train my eyes to see as God sees with the love with which God loves, it is hard to look with lust.

Q5. (Matthew 5:27-30) The spirit of our age is very accepting and approving of lust. According to Jesus' words, how seriously are we to take lust? How does agape love help us combat lust?
http://www.joyfulheart.com/forums/index.php?showtopic=748

Can you train your eyes? Can you train yourself to substitute your prurient gaze for one that sees the inner person whom God loves? Yes, with the Spirit of God in you to fulfill the spirit of the law, you can indeed. You'll need to break the habit of lust, perhaps, and that is difficult. But you *can* learn to look with love. And that, my friends, is how Jesus looks.

Prayer

Lord Jesus. Train our eyes to look with your love. Forgive us our lust and selfishness and shame. And remake us in the image of our Master. In your power we pray. Amen.

Excursus 4: Homosexual Lust

In response to my teaching on "looking lustfully" (Matthew 5:27-30), I received this question:

"Am I correct in interpreting your words as saying that God accepts homosexual love?"
– Joanne

Here is my response:

Dear Joanne,

Here in California, where I live, when people talk about homosexual love, they are talking about sexual desire for someone of the same sex. I don't believe that God accepts homosexual lust, that is, a burning sexual desire for a member of the same sex. No more than he accepts heterosexual lust, burning sexual desire for one you are not married to. They are both wrong and damning.

But I believe God can enable those who have homosexual leanings to learn how to love purely with "agape" love. Just as he can help those heterosexuals burning up with lust for women who not their wives to learn to love women in a pure way.

Each of us has different weaknesses. Perhaps 3% to 5% of men seem to have a sexual attraction to other men and develop a lifestyle characterized by homosexual lust. A much larger percentage of men have a serious problem giving into heterosexual lusts. These are both weaknesses. Both are "abnormal" if we define "normal" as the way God has created us to be – whole.

But our God is a freeing, delivering, redeeming God. The wonder of the Gospel is that he loves us. As messed up as we are, he loves us. And more than that, he has extended himself way beyond what we deserve in order to pull us up from the dregs of sin in which we have lived.

"He himself bore our sins in his own body on the tree, so that we might die to sins and live for righteousness. By his wounds we have been healed!" (1 Peter 2:24)

The gospel is good news to sexual addicts of all stripes – whether lust in the heart or acted out lust. For it tells us that, finally, we are *accepted*.

"Accept one another, then, just as Christ accepted you." (Romans 15:7)

This does not mean that our sins are acceptable. They are not. But that our sins, even the deep sins of the heart, are cleansed and forgiven through Christ's sacrifice for us, and so we are *accepted*.

If we can believe the Gospel that God accepts us, it will begin to remove the intense sense of shame and guilt that we feel. This will begin to evaporate as we lay hold of the truth. And a clear conscience will gradually be restored (Hebrews 10:22).

And as our minds are renewed, and we begin to cooperate with the Holy Spirit to reject lust and strive for real love, agape love, our hearts will be purified by the Holy Spirit. This is a process of renewal (theologically we call this "sanctification") that doesn't happen overnight. But it *does* happen.

The Gospel of Jesus Christ is more powerful than lust! That is good news!

Incidentally, for those who are struggling with homosexuality, there is a wonderful Christian organization called Exodus International (www.exodusinternational.org) with chapters in many cities. Research has found that the approach Exodus uses has brought substantial though modest evidence of change in many individuals.[1]

---

[1] Tim Stafford, "The Best Research Yet," *Christianity Today*, September 13, 2007 (www.ctlibrary.com/49779). Discusses the findings of Stanton L. Jones and Mark A. Yarhouse, *Ex-Gays? A Longitudinal Study of Religiously Mediated Change in Sexual Orientation* (InterVarsity Press Academic, 2007).

5. The Spirit of Marriage. Jesus' Teaching on Divorce (5:27-32 with Matthew 19:1-12)

It is difficult to teach on divorce because it seems to bring to the surface all the pain that people of our generation carry. And when there is pain there is sensitivity, extreme sensitivity to anything that might be construed as judgmental. If Jesus were to speak publicly today about divorce he would be lambasted as being politically incorrect, judgmental, harsh, and unbending. He would be silenced because his words would be too painful to a generation that has suffered so much hurt from divorce.

But perhaps Jesus' teaching carries with it the seeds of truth that we need to heal us. Perhaps if we embrace Jesus' teaching in spite of our pain, and pass his words on to the next generation, they will do better than we. Let's examine his teaching.

Raphael, detail of "Marriage of the Virgin" (1504), after Perugino, Oil on panel. Pinacoteca di Brera, Milan.

In this section we're looking at Jesus' brief words on divorce in the Sermon on the Mount.

> "It has been said, 'Anyone who divorces his wife must give her a certificate of divorce.' But I tell you that anyone who divorces his wife, except for marital unfaithfulness, causes her to become an adulteress, and anyone who marries the divorced woman commits adultery." (5:31-32)

It is difficult to deal with so complex a subject with these two verses alone. Why does Jesus say this? What is behind it? Jesus offers a more extended teaching on divorce in Matthew 19:3-12, so this chapter will consider carefully what he teaches there. As we study, we'll begin to understand what Jesus intended in the spirit of marriage.

> "3 Some Pharisees came to him to test him. They asked, 'Is it lawful for a man to divorce his wife for any and every reason?'
>
> 4 'Haven't you read,' he replied, 'that at the beginning the Creator "made them male and female," 5 and said, "For this reason a man will leave his father and mother and be united to his wife, and the two will become one flesh"? 6 So they are no longer two, but one. Therefore what God has joined together, let man not separate.'
>
> 7 'Why then,' they asked, 'did Moses command that a man give his wife a certificate of divorce and send her away?'
>
> 8 Jesus replied, 'Moses permitted you to divorce your wives because your hearts were hard. But it was not this way from the beginning. 9 I tell you that anyone who divorces his wife, except for marital unfaithfulness, and marries another woman commits adultery.'" (Matthew 19:3-9)

Various Interpretations

We must recognize at the onset that there have been several interpretations of Jesus' teaching by various branches the Christian Church. The major positions are:

1. **Divorce, but not remarriage, is permitted in the case of unchastity**. This is the view of the majority of the early church fathers, Roman Catholics, and many evangelicals.

2. **Divorce is not permitted in any case; unchastity is not an exception**. A few evangelicals.

3. **Both divorce and remarriage are permitted in cases of unchastity and desertion**. This is the view of most of the Protestant Reformers and many evangelicals.

4. **Divorce in the case of unlawful marriages is permitted**. This position is widely accepted and provides the basis for the Roman Catholic practice of annulment.

No matter what way I interpret this passage, there will be a sizeable number of readers who will disagree with me. This is kind of like treading a theological minefield, and there is no way that I can fully treat the subject or support fully my own understanding in the space I have. My goal, however, is to help us to understand what Jesus taught and what is the spirit of marriage that lies behind Jesus' teaching.

Challenge from the Pharisees (Matthew 19:3)

Now let's examine Jesus' teaching in Matthew 19 in some detail.

"Some Pharisees came to him to test him. They asked, 'Is it lawful for a man to divorce his wife for any and every reason?'" (19:3)

In the Middle East in ancient times divorce was common and taken for granted. This already widespread practice was regulated and therefore limited by Deuteronomy 24:1-4. The key verse reads:

> "If a man marries a woman who becomes displeasing to him because he finds something indecent about her, and he writes her a certificate of divorce, gives it to her and sends her from his house...." (Deuteronomy 24:1)

The Mosaic Law provided that a husband could not just send his wife away casually. There was the requirement that the husband must write out a legal document called a "certificate of divorce" and give it to his wife (and then forfeit his wife's dowry, which made divorce too expensive for most husbands).[1]

The allowable cause for the divorce, "because he finds something indecent about her" (NIV, verse 1) was hotly debated – in Jesus' day and in ours. Literally, the word means "nakedness of a thing" and may be a technical term. We just aren't sure of its exact meaning.[2]

In Matthew 19:1-12, the Pharisees are asking their question about divorce "to test him," trying to put Jesus on the spot, to force him to take a controversial stand that would alienate people. The Pharisees themselves didn't even agree on the answer. The more lenient rabbinical school of Hillel interpreted Deuteronomy 24:1 as allowing divorce for any reason, even a wife spoiling her husband's dinner. As a result of this interpretation, divorce was widespread in Jesus' day.[3] But this was still an issue of debate, since the stricter school of Shammai believed that the term in Deuteronomy referred only to unchastity.[4]

In the Beginning (Matthew 19:4-6)

In answering the Pharisees, Jesus goes back to God's original intention for marriage as found in two passages in Genesis:

> "So God created man in his own image,
> in the image of God he created him;
> male and female he created them." (Genesis 1:27)

---

[1] J.A. Thompson, *Deuteronomy* (Tyndale Old Testament Commentaries; InterVarsity Press, 1974), p. 244.

[2] Thompson, *Deuteronomy*, pp. 243-245. Peter C. Craigie, *Deuteronomy* (New International Commentary on the Old Testament; Eerdmans, 1976), pp. 304-306.

[3] David Instone-Brewer, "What God Has Joined," *Christianity Today*, October 2007, pp. 26-29.

[4] Leon Morris, *Matthew* (Eerdmans, 1992), pp. 479-480. George Foot Moore, *Judaism* (Hendrickson, 1927, reprinted 1997), volume 2, pp. 119ff.

> "For this reason a man will leave his father and mother and be united to his wife, and they will become one flesh." (Genesis 2:24)

Then Jesus goes on to interpret these verses (Matthew 19:6):

> "So they are no longer two, but one. Therefore what God has joined together, let man not separate."

In other words, God has made the man and woman one. God has joined them and it isn't for man to sever the union.

Q1. (Matthew 5:27-32; 19:1-12) With whom did Jesus side: Rabbi Hillel or Rabbi Shammai? What exception does Jesus give to his prohibition of divorce? How does this exception relate to Deuteronomy 24:1-4?
http://www.joyfulheart.com/forums/index.php?showtopic=749

What God Has Joined (19:6)

One question I am commonly asked is framed something like this: "My first wife and I weren't married in a church, so we were never married in the eyes of God, were we?" My answer goes back to the beginning, too. God instituted marriage and made a man and his wife one flesh. It had nothing especially to do with church or religion. It had to do with God's institution of marriage, a kind of "natural law" based on God's intention for marriage and the way he made human beings.

The Apostle Paul draws on this natural law when he says,

> "Do you not know that he who unites himself with a prostitute is one with her in body?
> For it is said, 'The two will become one flesh.'" (1 Corinthians 6:16)

Even an illicit union involves this essential unity or "one flesh" relationship between a man and a woman.

Men and women can be "just friends," but when they have sex the relationship changes significantly. They view each other differently. They have shared something that unites them. Pulling that bond apart is wrenching, damaging. No wonder that the casual sex so acceptable in our generation can weaken subsequent marriages.

Homosexuality

Jesus doesn't discuss homosexuality in Matthew 19, but his teaching on God joining a man and a woman in marriage is germane. Homosexuality is a perversion of God's intention for the one flesh relationship between a man and a woman. Women can have strong and deep friendships with other women. Men can have strong and deep friendships with other men. That is good and healthy. But these should not be confused with sexual relationships. Sexual relationships are something else entirely and involve spiritual and social relationships that cannot be perverted without serious consequences to the individual, the family, and the society. (See Excursus 4, "Homosexual Lust," in chapter 5 above.)

So in his teaching, Jesus doesn't appeal to one rabbi or another. He goes back to God's original intention for marriage "in the beginning." And he concludes that God's intention for marriage is that the man and woman be joined in an indissoluble union, "one flesh."

Q2. (Matthew 19:4-6 quoting Genesis 2:24) Do people need to be Christians to be joined as one flesh? Is this making into "one flesh" accomplished by a religious ceremony or by natural law? Of those who have entered into a first marriage, what percentage do you think have been "joined together" by God, according to Jesus' statement in Matthew 19:6?
http://www.joyfulheart.com/forums/index.php?showtopic=750

Certificate of Divorce (Matthew 19:7)

The Pharisees aren't happy with this answer, however, since their purpose is to hold Jesus' feet over the fire of controversy. What are the allowable causes for divorce? they want to know. So they ask another question.

> 7 "'Why then,' they asked, 'did Moses command that a man give his wife a certificate of divorce and send her away?'
>
> 8 Jesus replied, 'Moses permitted you to divorce your wives because your hearts were hard. But it was not this way from the beginning. 9 I tell you that anyone who divorces his wife, except for marital unfaithfulness, and marries another woman commits adultery.'" (Matthew 19:7-9)

Notice the spin the Pharisees put on the question. "Why did Moses command...?" Moses didn't command divorce. What he *did* command is that if a man wanted to divorce his wife, he couldn't just turn her out of her house. It had to be a formal and legal severing of the marriage, with financial implications as well as the ability to remarry. Without a certificate of divorce, the wife would not be able to remarry.

This, of course, is one of the big questions we ask. Can a divorced person remarry? In the society of Jesus' day the answer was Yes. Divorce and the right to remarry went hand in hand with each other. Divorce was usually performed by saying, "You are free to marry any man."[5]

Because of Your Hardness of Heart (Matthew 19:8)

But Jesus does not accept the Pharisees' objection that Moses permitted divorce. Jesus asserts:

> "Moses permitted you to divorce your wives because your hearts were hard. But it was not that way from the beginning" (Matthew 19:8).

In other words, Jesus says that divorce is an accommodation to the sinfulness of man's heart – not part of God's original plan.

What kind of hardness of heart does he have in mind? Selfishness, self-centeredness, I presume. Look at marriages today. Where does the trouble arise? Often it comes from the self-centeredness of the husband – or the self-absorption of the wife – and their subsequent lack of communicating with each other.

In March 1999, Barbara Walters interviewed Monica Lewinski who admitted to a sexual relationship with then U.S. President Bill Clinton. During the previous year she had gone through an extremely difficult time, but now she wanted to resurrect her image and tell her story to the world. Miss Walters led her through events step by step, and Monica replied in her own words. As I watched, I was struck by how she related everything about her relationship with the President to how it affected her – and her alone. In many ways she was likeable, personable, and attractive, but extremely self-absorbed. One of the network commentators described it as narcissism, a word derived from the story of the beautiful youth in Greek mythology who pines away for love of his own reflection and is then turned into a narcissus flower. Unfortunately self-centeredness is all too common in marriages.

How can you have a marriage in which one spouse is self-absorbed, selfish? The other spouse has to do all the giving while the self-absorbed one does all the receiving. That's bad enough. What do you do when both spouses are self-absorbed? This is the opposite of love. It is the hardness of heart that Jesus was describing.

---

[5] *Gittin* 9.3; quoted in Robert H. Stein, "Divorce," DJG, p. 193.

Q3. (Matthew 19:7-8) According to Jesus, does the Mosaic law command divorce? Does it allow or regulate it? Why does it allow divorce at all? What was God's original intention ("from the beginning") for marriage and divorce, according to Jesus?
http://www.joyfulheart.com/forums/index.php?showtopic=751

Love is the Fulfilling of the Law

How can you fulfill God's intention for marriage? Love, self-giving love. Love is the fulfilling of the Law, Jesus said (Matthew 20:37-40). And love is the only way a marriage can work for a lifetime. Love is the only way to fulfill the law. Jesus said it, and when you think about it, it is self-evident.

The Apostle Paul told husbands, "Love your wives, just as Christ loved the church and gave himself up for her..." (Ephesians 5:25). He went on to expound on the one flesh relationship that Jesus also saw as the root of the marriage relationship. "Husbands ought to love their wives as their own bodies," Paul teaches. "He who loves his wife loves himself...." Paul goes on to quote Genesis 2:24.

God made marriage to run on the basis of love. Not erotic, romantic love only, but self-giving, self-sacrificing love. Paul compares the agape love of Christ who gave himself up for us to the love that should exist in a marriage. God made law and society and relationships to run on love, too. Yes, there must be a provision for the case of sin – murder, stealing, hardness of heart. But the essence, the root principle, is love and lifelong unity.

But I Tell You .... (Matthew 19:9)

Jesus contrasts what the religious leaders were saying about Moses and a certificate of divorce with his own pronouncement:

> "I tell you that anyone who divorces his wife, except for marital unfaithfulness, and marries another woman commits adultery" (Matthew 19:9).

What Jesus said to the Pharisees was radical indeed. They were arguing about how big the escape hatch was. But Jesus was saying, in essence, that there is no escape hatch from God's intention of lifelong marriage. And to divorce and remarry was to commit adultery.

Wow! Just like each of the elements of the Sermon on the Mount, he contrasts, "You have heard it said ..." with "but I say to you." The legalism is contrasted with the spirit of the law.

There are a lot of adulterers out there. Oh, not guilty of the act of adultery, perhaps. It takes the shape of looking on a woman with adulterous intent, or divorcing one woman and marrying another. But Jesus says that the heart of the problem is desiring someone who does not belong to you. God's intent is treating people with love not lust, and with faithfulness not selfishness. The fulfillment of the Law is love.

The Apostle Paul echoes this understanding of Jesus' words:

> "To the married I give this command (not I, but the Lord): A wife must not separate from her husband. But if she does, she must remain unmarried or else be reconciled to her husband. And a husband must not divorce his wife." (1 Corinthians 7:10-11)

For Jesus and Paul, the spirit of marriage and its one-flesh unity forbid divorce. But even in Paul's command, there is room for man's hardness of heart. "A wife must not separate from her husband," he says. "But if she does ...." Sometimes separation is necessary – for safety of a spouse and children, for example. The "separation" in verse 10 apparently refers to divorce, since Paul speaks of remaining unmarried. But it is divorce without the freedom to remarry, since that would preclude reconciliation, which is at the heart of God's intention for husband and wife.

Better Not to Marry (Matthew 19:10-11)

Jesus' disciples got the point loud and clear.

> "The disciples said to him, 'If this is the situation between a husband and wife, it is better not to marry.'" (Matthew 19:10).

They were saying, "If there's no escape hatch allowed at all, then we'd better not marry at all."

Jesus' reply is interesting. He says,

> "Not everyone can accept this word, but only those to whom it has been given." (Matthew 19:11)

The key issue for interpreting this verse is whether "this word" refers to what precedes it about divorce, or what comes after it, about being a eunuch for the kingdom of heaven. Which is the teaching that everyone can't accept? The no divorce part or the eunuch part? In fact, people have trouble accepting either. I expect, however, that Jesus was referring to marriage in general – that many couldn't accept Jesus' teaching about God's intention for marriage.

Q4. (Matthew 19:10) Why do you think Jesus' disciples reacted so negatively to his teaching on marriage and divorce? Did they misunderstand it?
http://www.joyfulheart.com/forums/index.php?showtopic=752

Eunuchs for the Kingdom of Heaven (Matthew 19:12)

> "For some are eunuchs because they were born that way; others were made that way by men; and others have renounced marriage because of the kingdom of heaven. The one who can accept this should accept it." (Matthew 19:12)

Jesus concludes this teaching on marriage by noting that some people give up marriage entirely in order to better serve the Kingdom of Heaven. This, too, was radical. The Judaism of Jesus' day saw marriage as the only way to fulfill the command to "be fruitful and multiply," and those who did not marry were looked down upon.

So Jesus introduces the concept that some people forgo marriage to carry out God plan for their lives. Not all, but some. Jesus, surely, was one of those people. Nothing is wrong with marriage, but it would have hindered him in his ministry. The Apostle Paul instructed disciples about the mutual responsibilities of the conjugal relationship, but then says,

> "I say this as a concession, not as a command. I wish that all men were as I am. But each man has his own gift from God; one has this gift, another has that." (1 Corinthians 7:6-7)

At this point in time, at least, Paul wasn't married. What wife would have put up with a husband who was gone for years at a time and was willing to live at a poverty level when necessary to advance the Gospel? Not many.

Protestants tend to be suspect of those who embrace voluntary celibacy. But there has been a strong movement towards religious celibacy of Christian workers in the Roman Catholic movement since the Third or Fourth Century. I disagree with my Catholic friends that priests *must* be unmarried (see 1 Timothy 3:2 and Titus 1:6), and that female Christian workers *must* take vows of celibacy (though see 1 Timothy 5:11-12, 14), but I admire and respect those who have taken this vow due to God's calling.

John Wesley (1703-1791) was one of those who *should* have taken a vow of celibacy. He was active in an itinerant ministry across England for many years. But when he was past 50, he decided to marry a widow. She tried to follow him on his incessant travels for the first couple of years, but broke down under it. After that she made his life utterly miserable. John Wesley was a gift to Christianity, but never should have married. It was a mistake.

An example of a celibate Christian worker who has changed the world's perception of Christian good works is Mother Teresa of Calcutta (1910-1997). Having no husband probably benefited her ability to carry out her ministry effectively. Her calling to the dying of Calcutta wasn't compatible with marriage and raising a family. She "became a eunuch for the kingdom of heaven" and was used marvelously by God.

Except for Marital Unfaithfulness ... (19:9)

Even in Jesus' sayings in Matthew's gospel we see an exception, "except for marital unfaithfulness," both in the Sermon on the Mount (5:32) and in his more extended teaching in 19:9. The word translated "fornication" (KJV) or "marital unfaithfulness" (NIV) is Greek *pornia*, which refers to "unlawful sexual intercourse, prostitution, unchastity, fornication."[6] We get our word "pornography" from this root. It is a broad word, covering all kinds of sexual misbehavior.

Some people deny that it could include adultery, since one was subject to the death penalty for that. But in Jesus' day, punishment by stoning for adultery was probably rare. A righteous person would divorce a spouse who was guilty of adultery (see, for example, Joseph, in Matthew 1:19). [7]

Others claim that the exception clause, "except for marital unfaithfulness," was not part of Jesus' original words. They argue that neither Mark 10:11-12, presumed to be the earliest gospel, nor Luke 16:18 include the exception. They suggest that it was added by early Christian scribes concerned that the words were too harsh by themselves. However, there is no manuscript evidence for this theory.

I don't want to second guess Matthew's Gospel. Jesus wasn't overturning the law that permitted divorce in cases of unchastity. That would be assumed by readers in first century Palestine, but Matthew includes the clause so there is no doubt of Jesus' intention. I don't want to put myself in a position to pick and choose among Jesus' words looking for the earliest as authentic. I accept Matthew's Gospel as authentically representing the teaching of Jesus.

I understand, then, that Jesus taught that "any cause divorce" that the school of Hillel

---

[6] *Porneia*, BDAG 854.

[7] Raymond E. Brown (*The Gospel According to John I-XII* (Doubleday, 1966), vol. 29A, p. 333) cites Blinzer as conclusive that stoning was still in practice in Jesus' time (J. Blinzler, "Die Strafe für Ehebruch in Bibel und Halacha zur Auslegung von Joh. viii 5," NTS 4 (1957-58), 32-47). On the other hand, Leon Morris (*The Gospel According to John* (New International Commentary on the New Testament; Eerdmans, 1971), p. 887, fn. 19) sites several sources that indicate divorce as a much more common result of adultery than stoning, citing Israel Abrahams, *Studies in Pharisaism and the Gospels*, First Series (Cambridge, 1917), pp. 73-74; and *Sotah* 5:1 in the Mishnah. See also Morris, *Matthew*, p. 121, fn. 122.

allowed was not permissible, except in the case of infidelity of one's spouse. But would the "innocent" spouse then be free to remarry? No, say some interpreters. I believe, however, that the "innocent" spouse *would* be free to remarry. If the divorce was permissible, along with it in first century Palestine was the permission to remarry. Jesus does not contradict this in Matthew.

Of course, we're now getting into the kind of legalistic hairsplitting that Jesus so abhorred. The Pharisees and the Judaism they represented had turned the faith into a complex system of case law. Jesus, on the other hand, wanted to teach his followers the heart and spirit of the Law – love.

Marital unfaithfulness can break the essential oneness that is to exist between husband and wife. When one of the partners becomes "one flesh" with someone not their spouse, something about their union with their spouse is broken and defiled. I am thankful that some marriages are able to survive adultery, but many are not able to. It is possible for love to overcome even this sin; I have seen marriages weather this blow, but it is all too rare. Jesus, I believe, allows the exception of marital unfaithfulness, since by its very nature it severs that "one flesh" bond that Jesus sees at the root of marriage.

An Exception for Desertion?

In his teaching to the Christian church at Corinth, Paul seems to introduce another exception. First, he affirms what Jesus taught. When Paul says, "To the married I give this command (not I, but the Lord)..." (1 Corinthians 7:10), he means believers. That was the situation Jesus addressed; Jesus was called to the Jews, believers in God.

But then Paul addresses another common situation in Corinth: Christians married to non-Christians. This is a different situation. Only one is under obedience to the Lord's teaching, not both. Paul begins by saying, "To the rest I say this (I, not the Lord)..." (1 Corinthians 7:12), meaning, "To the rest of the believers in Corinth I say on my own authority as an apostle, not by the direct words of Jesus...."

Paul teaches them:

> "To the rest I say this (I, not the Lord): If any brother has a wife who is not a believer and she is willing to live with him, he must not divorce her. And if a woman has a husband who is not a believer and he is willing to live with her, she must not divorce him.... But if the unbeliever leaves, let him do so. A believing man or woman is not bound in such circumstances; God has called us to live in peace. How do you know, wife, whether you will save your husband? Or, how do you know, husband, whether you will save your wife?" (1 Corinthians 7:12-16)

Paul seems to allow divorce when a non-believing spouse leaves or deserts a believing spouse. Moreover, he also seems to allow remarriage, since he says, "A believing man or woman is not bound (*douloō*) in such circumstances." I take Paul's teaching on divorce of a non-believing spouse from a believing spouse that the believer is now free from the marriage and can remarry.

Such a view has been reinforced in recent years by David Instone-Brewer, a New Testament scholar who has carefully researched Jewish marriage and divorce practices in Jesus' day. He concludes that Jesus' prohibition on divorce "for any cause" dealt with his interpretation of Deuteronomy 24:1 only, not the provision of Exodus 21:10-11, generally accepted in Jesus' day, which allowed for divorce in cases where a spouse was deprived of food, clothing, and marital rights.[8]

> "If he takes another wife to himself, he shall not diminish the food, clothing, or marital rights of the first wife. And if he does not do these three things for her, she shall go out without debt, without payment of money." (Exodus 21:10-11)

Application of the Principle

We've spent a good deal of time examining what the Scripture teaches. How are we to apply it then as we live in the midst of "an adulterous and sinful generation"? Carefully and lovingly.

We need to clearly understand that God's intention is that marriage be enduring. When we enter into marriage, we do so without any escape clause. We do so with faith in God and a firm commitment to love our spouse as our own body. It is a joyous relationship often, but also a self-sacrificing and demanding one. We must teach our children and our brothers and sisters in our churches what God says about marriage.

However, while we honor marriage with all that is in us, we must also recognize man's hardness of heart. We will have in our fellowship people whose marriages have been broken by adultery, by desertion, by selfishness, by unfaithfulness. And we must love them. "Above all, love each other deeply, because love covers over a multitude of sins" (1 Peter 4:8). Sometimes I struggle as a pastor to try both:

1. To uphold the standard and sanctity of marriage, and
2. To love and heal the hurt and fallen.

Jesus faced the same struggle that we do – and his interpretation of the Law certainly

[8] David Instone-Brewer, "What God Has Joined," *Christianity Today*, October 2007, pp. 26-29. Instone-Brewer, a research fellow in rabbinics and the New Testament at Tyndale House, Cambridge, has published several books on the subject, including *Divorce and Remarriage in the Church: Biblical Solutions for Pastoral Realities* (InterVarsity Press, 2006) and *Divorce and Remarriage in the Bible: The Social and Literary Context* (Eerdmans, 2002)

didn't please everyone. Among the legalistic Pharisees he was considered too soft, too merciful. But to his disciples he inspired awe and holiness, "Depart from me, for I am a sinful man, O Lord."

Practical Considerations

Does a person who has remarried after a divorce that wasn't caused by marital unfaithfulness, live in a perpetual state of adultery? Should that person divorce or separate in order to get back into God's will, or is getting back into God's will no longer possible? There are some things that can shatter the marriage bond irretrievably. One of those, I believe, is marital unfaithfulness.

So what about the person who divorces and remarries and so commits adultery? Is that adultery perpetual? No, I don't believe so. Yes, there is adultery, but that adultery breaks whatever may have remained of the marriage bond of the first marriage. There is sin. Grievous sin. But when that marriage bond is once broken and there is no repairing the first marriage, the adultery is past, too. I don't counsel Christians who find themselves in a wrong second marriage to leave their current spouses and go back to the first spouses – even if that were possible. (That was prohibited, apparently, by Deuteronomy 24:3-4.)

Instead, repent from the heart, ask forgiveness from God and those you have wronged, and live out your life in Christ in the present marriage. I've seen God bless some second marriages that certainly began in gross sin. God is gracious, though we are responsible for our actions and sins. I've also seen some disastrous second marriages. More of the latter than of the former.

Let's say a Christian husband separates from his Christian wife and divorces her. She is not free to marry, nor is he, according to 1 Corinthians 7:10-11 and Matthew 19:9. But if he moves in with a girlfriend, whether or not he marries her, the situation seems to change. He is now guilty of unfaithfulness to the marriage bond between him and his first wife, and he is committing adultery. His action shatters the marriage bond. His first wife, I believe, is now free to marry if God so guides her.

Sadly, even supposed Christians are so quick to begin dating as soon as they are separated, that many forestall by their adultery the reconciliation that God desires for them.

Warning. Believing Christians disagree on some aspects of divorce and remarriage. In addition, many have been hurt in bad marriages and divorces. Be gentle, sensitive, and loving with one another – even if you disagree!

Q5. (Matthew 19:9) Does a person who has remarried after a divorce that wasn't caused by marital unfaithfulness, live in a perpetual state of adultery? Should that person divorce or separate in order to get back into God's will? How can he or she get back into God's will, or is that no longer possible?
http://www.joyfulheart.om/forums/index.php?showtopic=753

My dear brothers and sisters, Jesus has shared his heart with us his disciples. God's intention, long prior to the giving of the Law, was for us to live with our spouse as "one flesh" for "as long as we both shall live." Self-giving love is not just a Christian add-on to the Law. It is the heart and soul of the Law. This one-flesh principal also becomes the basis of Paul's teaching of the "marriage" of Christ and his Church, won by sacrificial agape love (Ephesians 5:21-33). Humans are quick to find an escape hatch that will allow them to wriggle free of marriage. That is the opposite of God's intent. The spirit of marriage that God has for you and me is love.

No matter what the adulterous and sinful world around us says is acceptable, our calling is a higher one. We seek to fulfill in our lives, so far we ourselves are able, the perfect will of God for our marriages. Even when we are having trouble in our marriages – especially at those times – we should be emboldened to pray, "Father, work out your perfect will in my life and that of my spouse. For Jesus' sake! Amen."

Prayer

Father, we humans have so often messed up your original plan for marriage and for our lives. Some are still grieving the ruins of a once-hopeful marriage. Others are children of divorce and have paid dearly for the divorces of their parents. Help us all in our brokenness. Heal our lives – and our marriages – we pray, with your powerful love. We confess our sins. Forgive and heal. We pray in Jesus' name. Amen.

Extra Credit

Q6. The Church has always been supportive of those who are hurting or scarred. In Christ, we help people make the best of what is sometimes a difficult situation. What can you do to extend Christ's healing love to someone who is struggling in his or her marriage? What can you do to bring healing to someone who is or was divorced?
http://www.joyfulheart.com/forums/index.php?showtopic=754

6. The Spirit of Truthfulness and Love (5:33-48)

"Don't swear at all," we read, and wonder if this applies to us. We don't use foul language, perhaps. We certainly don't take oaths by Jerusalem. Why include something this obscure in the Sermon on the Mount?

Because the point of Jesus' words is the Spirit of Making Promises, and that applies in every age. To understand what Jesus was saying, we need to begin in the Old Testament.

Oath Taking in the Old Testament

A number of places in the Old Testament, people were warned to keep the vows they made when they invoked the name of the LORD.

Photo copyright clipart.com

> "You shall not misuse the name of the LORD your God, for the LORD will not hold anyone guiltless who misuses his name." (Exodus 20:7)

> "Do not swear falsely by my name and so profane the name of your God. I am the LORD." (Leviticus 19:12)

> "When a man makes a vow to the LORD or takes an oath to obligate himself by a pledge, he must not break his word but must do everything he said." (Numbers 30:2)

> "If you make a vow to the LORD your God, do not be slow to pay it, for the LORD your God will certainly demand it of you and you will be guilty of sin." (Deuteronomy 23:21)

Since ancient times, especially in legal situations, people were required to take an oath in the name of their deity, as a way of testifying to their truthfulness. The idea was that if you swear by what you hold holy and are telling a lie, then your deity will surely punish you.

As the King James Version puts the Third Commandment this way:

> "Thou shalt not take the name of the Lord thy God in vain" (Exodus 20:7)

In other words, if you use the name of your holy God in an oath, you'd better keep it. Otherwise your words are empty.

A number of times God swears an oath by his own reputation and holiness. The ceremony we see in Genesis 15:12-21 is an ancient ceremony of "cutting" a covenant and swearing to the other party to keep it. Joseph speaks of the land that God "promised on oath to Abraham, Isaac and Jacob" (Genesis 50:24). See also Hebrews 4:3 (quoting Psalm 95:11), and Hebrews 6:13, where the writer says, "When God made his promise to Abraham, since there was no one greater for him to swear by, he swore by himself."

Occasions for Oaths

We have a similar custom in our day. When someone is inducted into office he or she is required to take an "oath of office" to "uphold the constitution ... so help me God." When a person gives testimony in court, he is required to promise "under oath" that what he says will be "the truth, the whole truth, and nothing but the truth, so help me God."

Under our laws, to lie "under oath" is to commit a grave crime, a felony, perjury, punishable by time in jail.

Pharisees' Perversion of Oaths

In order not to use the actual name of Yahweh "in vain," the Jews developed the habit of substituting another word in its place: "LORD," "heaven," etc. But were these substitute words of sufficient holiness to make the oath binding? The Pharisees, the strict religious elite of their day, had made a mockery of oath-taking. They took frivolous oaths, designed to mislead the hearers. Later in the Gospel of Matthew, Jesus severely castigates them for how they use an appearance of truth-telling to deceive and mislead:

> "Woe to you, blind guides! You say, 'If anyone swears by the temple, it means nothing; but if anyone swears by the gold of the temple, he is bound by his oath.' You blind fools! Which is greater: the gold, or the temple that makes the gold sacred? You also say, 'If anyone swears by the altar, it means nothing; but if anyone swears by the gift on it, he is bound by his oath.' You blind men! Which is greater: the gift, or the altar that makes the gift sacred? Therefore, he who swears by the altar swears by it and by everything on it. And he who swears by the temple swears by it and by the one who dwells in it. And he who swears by heaven swears by God's throne and by the one who sits on it." (Matthew 23:16-22)

They had developed a complicated system to determine which oaths were and were not binding. In the Jewish code of law called the *Mishnah*, there is an entire tractate devoted to the validity of oaths. Jesus tells his followers,

> "Do not swear at all: either by heaven, for it is God's throne; or by the earth, for it is his footstool; or by Jerusalem, for it is the city of the Great King." (5:34-35)

Why? Because there is no difference in holiness between heaven, or earth, or Jerusalem! They are all equally God's, and equally holy. He was calling the Pharisees' intricate system of oaths what it was – a sham.

Don't Swear at All (5:34)

Jesus' answer to this foolishness? Don't take oaths at all!

When I was a boy when we wanted someone to believe us, we'd say something like, "I swear on a stack of Bibles!" or "Cross my heart and hope to die." These days, the young men in our church tell me, that you say something like, "I sweaaaar!"

But why should we invoke the deity to get someone to believe us? To even feel the need to do so tells us how our credibility has fallen. As A.M. Hunter puts it, "Oaths arise because men are so often liars."[1] Jesus says that we aren't to resort to oaths in order to be believed.

Let Your "Yes" Mean "Yes" (5:37a)

He says, "Simply let your 'Yes' be 'Yes,' and your 'No,' 'No' " (5:37).

In other words, don't play games to deceive with your words. Let your words be plainly true themselves.

So easily we fall into word games. In 1998, President Clinton became famous for his careful definition of the word "is" and "sexual relations," words he used with his own private definitions with the intent to deceive, but with the demeanor of one who was telling the truth.

What would Jesus say to this? "Say what you mean!" Not that we have to blab everything we know. We need to be discrete, and make sure we are "speaking the truth in love" (Ephesians 4:15), but we need to speak the truth.

More Than This Comes from the Evil One (5:37b)

Jesus attributes attempts to use deceitful speech to the evil one, Satan, who is a liar. In one of his confrontations with the Pharisees, Jesus told them:

> "You belong to your father, the devil, and you want to carry out your father's desire. He was a murderer from the beginning, not holding to the truth, for there is no truth in him. When he lies, he speaks his native language, for he is a liar and the father of lies." (John 8:44)

When we use language to deceive, we are following the devil, not our Lord.

---

[1] Archibald M. Hunter, *A Pattern for Life* (Westminster Press, 1953), p. 51.

Q1. (Matthew 5:33-37) What does it mean: Let your "yes" be yes and your "no" be no? If we obeyed this command, what would be the result in our speaking? In our credibility?

http://www.joyfulheart.com/forums/index.php?showtopic=755

Practical Application

We need to be plain-spoken people who mean what we say and say what we mean. Sure, we'll make some people angry in the process. We can't please everyone, and when we try to please everyone, we catch the politician's disease of promising people whatever they desire with no intention of keeping our promises. Do we want to be classed in the same echelon of credibility as used car salesmen and politicians? Then we need to be plain-spoken. People will respect us far more if they know they can trust what we say, even if they disagree, than if they take us for slick-talking deceivers.

A good test of our credibility starts at home. When you promise your spouse you'll do something, does he or she believe you? Does your child believe you? Our credibility depends upon our follow-through. We shouldn't have to take an oath to feel obligated to fulfill our word. When we make a promise, Jesus teaches us, we must mean it and fulfill it – without resorting to some kind of impressive-sounding oath. Jesus' band of followers were called to be Promise Keepers.

The reason Jesus included this section on oath-taking in the Sermon on the Mount is because learning to speak the truth is essential if we are to be disciples of The Way, The Truth, and The Life. If we would be his followers, we must speak truth like he does.

And love fulfills the law, because love does not deceive but honors another person enough to be honest with him. You'd want to know the truth, no matter how painful. Speak truth to your neighbor in the same way as you'd like to have truth told to you yourself. Love him as you love yourself. Love her as you love yourself.

Refuse to Take an Oath?

Finally, we need to examine how far we are to take this refusal to take oaths. Some sincere religious groups such as Anabaptists and Quakers refuse to take an oath; instead they insist on "affirming" something, in order to contentiously keep Jesus' command here. Is that what he had in mind? Are we to take this literally?

I don't believe so. His point was to end the foolish vowing that was a way to deceive someone. He wanted his disciples to speak the truth consistently so that they would be believed without an elaborate oath. He wanted their word to be their bond.

I don't believe we need to refuse to swear when required to do so in a court or similar situation. Jesus himself didn't. When he was in a mock trial at the high priest's house, he was required to speak under oath:

> "Then the high priest stood up and said to Jesus, 'Are you not going to answer? What is this testimony that these men are bringing against you?' But Jesus remained silent.
>
> The high priest said to him, 'I charge you under oath by the living God: Tell us if you are the Christ, the Son of God.'
>
> 'Yes, it is as you say,' Jesus replied. 'But I say to all of you: In the future you will see the Son of Man sitting at the right hand of the Mighty One and coming on the clouds of heaven.'" (Matthew 26:62-64)

Paul, too, sometimes calls God as his witness (Romans 1:9; 2 Corinthians 1:23; Philippians 1:8; 1 Thessalonians 2:5, 10). The point is not a legalistic one – a legalistic parsing of words is what Jesus was trying to combat! Jesus' word, "Do not swear at all," is intended as a solemn command to his disciples to speak truthfully without having to resort to any device to prop up their believability.

As John Stott concludes,

> "If divorce is due to human hard-heartedness, swearing is due to human untruthfulness. Both were permitted by the law; neither was commanded; neither should be necessary."[2]

We Christians are called not to oath-taking but to truth-telling. Not just on solemn occasions but every day, in every situation, so that we might reflect Jesus' truthfulness and his love for everyone around us.

The Spirit of Love versus Retaliation (5:38-48)

The second part of the passage we're looking at in this chapter may seem contradictory and impractical on the surface.

> "If someone strikes you on the right cheek, turn to him the other also." (5:39)

How can that be right? How can that be responsible? What is Jesus getting at? What does he mean?

---

[2] Stott, *The Message of the Sermon on the Mount*, p. 101.

An Eye for an Eye (5:38)

Perhaps we should start at the beginning. As he has in the previous reinterpretations of the Law, Jesus begins by stating what the Pharisees were fond of stating:

> "You have heard that it was said, 'Eye for eye, and tooth for tooth.'" But I tell you...."(5:38)

This is an ancient command, quoting from Exodus 21:24; Leviticus 24:20; and Deuteronomy 19:21.

At first glance it seems almost vindictive. If you hurt me, then I have a right to hurt you. If you put my eye out, I have a legal right to put yours out. But to see it this way is surely a misunderstanding of the ancient Near East. Two things we must understand about this famous *lex talionis*, "law of retaliation." First, it was designed to restrain man's vindictiveness, and second it was designed to be administered as the justice of a formal court.

James J. Tissot, "Cain Leadeth Abel to Death" (1896), watercolor, Jewish Museum, New York.

1. Restraint

We need to go back to the days when there was no police force. When someone injured you, your first angry reaction was to go and injure him. And not just to the extent that he injured you. Hurt him so badly that he'll never forget it. Crush him. Humiliate him. Destroy him. Anger is vile when it is aroused.

The *lex talionis*, "law of retaliation," simply stated says that you may not extract from someone who has injured you any more than you have lost. In other words, the punishment should fit the crime – no more, no less. Modern jurisprudence is based solidly on this sort of principle. Such a law didn't begin with Moses. We find it first in the ancient *Code of Hammurabi*, a king who ruled in Babylon from 1728 to 1686 BC.

> §196: If a seignior has destroyed the eye of a member of the aristocracy, they shall destroy his eye. [Seigneur is "a man of rank or authority; especially, the feudal lord of a manor."]

> §197: If he has broken a(nother) seignior's bone, they shall break his bone.

> §198: If he has destroyed the eye of a commoner or broken the bone of a commoner, he

shall pay one mina of silver.

§199: If he has destroyed the eye of a seignior's slave or broken the bone of a seignior's slave, he shall pay one-half his value.

§200: If a seignior has knocked out a tooth of a seignior of his own rank, they shall knock out his tooth.

§201: If a seignior has knocked out a commoner's tooth, he shall pay one-third mina of silver.[3]

The point here is to restrain man's vindictiveness, not encourage it.

2. Judicial Administration

Look again at section 200 of the *Code of Hammurabi:* "... they shall knock out his tooth." Who are "they" referred to here? Obviously it is the court that is administering the punishment, not the individual who was injured.

Look at the context of the "eye for an eye" passage and you see the same thing:

"One witness is not enough to convict a man accused of any crime or offense he may have committed. A matter must be established by the testimony of two or three witnesses. If a malicious witness takes the stand to accuse a man of a crime, the two men involved in the dispute must stand in the presence of the Lord before the priests and the judges who are in office at the time. The judges must make a thorough investigation, and if the witness proves to be a liar, giving false testimony against his brother, then do to him as he intended to do to his brother. You must purge the evil from among you. The rest of the people will hear of this and be afraid, and never again will such an evil thing be done among you. Show no pity: life for life, eye for eye, tooth for tooth, hand for hand, foot for foot." Deuteronomy 19:15-21

Clearly, the context is a court of law giving sentence. We see the same thing in Exodus 21:22-25. This is judicial punishment decided by a court. As John Stott puts it:

"It thus had the double effect of defining justice and restraining revenge. It also prohibited the taking of the law into one's own hands by the ghastly vengeance of the family feud."[4]

---

[3] Quoted in James B. Pritchard (editor), *The Ancient Near East,* (Princeton University Press, 1958), p. 161, § 195-201.

[4] Stott, *The Message of the Sermon on the Mount,* p. 104

Q2. (Exodus 21:24; Leviticus 24:20; Deuteronomy 19:15-21) What was the purpose of the "Eye for eye, and tooth for tooth" regulation? Is this law designed to be administered by a court or judge, or by an individual? Is it designed to govern judicial action or personal action?

http://www.joyfulheart.com/forums/index.php?showtopic=756

Pharisees' Interpretation

But the Pharisees of Jesus' time had twisted this law. Apparently, they had wrenched it from its judicial context and were applying it to justify their own personal actions. They had similarly misinterpreted Leviticus 19:18, since Jesus restates their interpretation:

> "You have heard that it was said, 'Love your neighbor and hate your enemy.'" (Matthew 5:43)

That may have been what the Pharisees said, but it wasn't what the scripture had said:

> "Do not hate your brother in your heart. Rebuke your neighbor frankly so you will not share in his guilt. Do not seek revenge or bear a grudge against one of your people, but love your neighbor as yourself. I am the Lord." (Leviticus 19:17-18)

Apparently, the Pharisees had twisted the scripture to allow themselves just the opposite: to personally retaliate against their enemies, to seek revenge, to bear a grudge.

Personal Non-Retaliation (5:39-42)

Until we grasp the Pharisees' twisting of the intent of Scripture, we won't be able to understand Jesus' words. Notice that Jesus' teaching here concerns personal and not judicial action:

> "But I tell you, Do not resist an evil person. If someone strikes you on the right cheek, turn to him the other also. And if someone wants to sue you and take your tunic, let him have your cloak as well. If someone forces you to go one mile, go with him two miles. Give to the one who asks you, and do not turn away from the one who wants to borrow from you." (5:39-42)

Jesus isn't placing his followers outside the protection of justice, but he is calling them to a higher standard. Instead of retaliation and resistance against enemies, he calls them to a radical love.

> "But I tell you: Love your enemies and pray for those who persecute you, that you may be sons of your Father in heaven. He causes his sun to rise on the evil and the good, and

sends rain on the righteous and the unrighteous." (5:44-45)

In other words, do good to your enemies – anyone can love friends.

Cameos (5:39-42)

The theme is non-retaliation. Jesus states the principle in verse 39a:

"Do not resist (*anthistēmi*) an evil person." (5:39a)

But perhaps "resist" is too easily misunderstood. It sounds like passivity in the face of evil. The Greek word is *anthistēmi*, which means literally, *anti*, "against" + *istēmi*, "put, set, place." It means "be in opposition to, set oneself against, oppose"[5] and carries the idea of hostility. You know the inner feeling that rises up when someone insults you or takes advantage of you. You automatically "set yourself against" that person in your heart. There is the outward resistance as well as the inward hardening towards that person. Jesus says: Do not set yourself against the evil person.

Then he illustrates this in four brief cameos or portraits. We need to be careful to see these as they were intended – as illustrations. They are not case law to serve as the basis of a new Christian legalism. They are examples – and striking examples at that:

1. "If someone strikes you on the right cheek, turn to him the other also" (verse 39b). A slap on the cheek refers to an insult more than an overt physical attack (2 Corinthians 11:20; John 18:22-23; Acts 23:2-5). It was a matter of honor that required appropriate financial recompense as damages.[6]

2. "And if someone wants to sue you and take your tunic, let him have your cloak as well" (verse 40). Though taking the cloak was prohibited on humanitarian grounds in the Old Testament law (Exodus 22:25-27; Deuteronomy 24:12-13), the disciple is to offer it freely. This is an example from law.

3. "If someone forces you to go one mile, go with him two miles" (verse 41). This is an allusion to the right of a Roman soldier to require a subject to carry his baggage one mile, highly resented as the prerogative of the oppressing army. Jesus counsels the disciple not only to renounce his rights, but to love his enemy.

4. "Give to the one who asks you, and do not turn away from the one who wants to borrow from you" (verse 42). While one couldn't obey this command literally for more than a few days without going broke, Jesus' point is that in the kingdom of

---

[5] *Anthistēmi*, BDAG 80.

[6] France, *Matthew*, p. 220. He cites m. *B. Qam.* 8:6 to the effect that a slap with the back of the hand was far more insulting and would entail double damages.

God self-interest doesn't rule, but rather love.

I am tempted to give a detailed explanation of each, but I don't think this is Jesus' intent. His point is clear. He wants us to do more than is required of us by our enemies, by those who are trying to use us, by those who are trying to take advantage of us. Rather than turn on them with resistance and retaliation we are to – in love for them – give them more than they require.

Q3. (Matthew 5:39-42) What do Jesus' examples or tiny cameos in verses 39-42 have in common? Someone has said that if we were to carry out verses 39-42 literally, we would aid and abet evil. Do you agree? How should we take these examples: As case law? As hyperbole? As a series of aphorisms or adages? In another way?
http://www.joyfulheart.com/forums/index.php?showtopic=757

Q4. (Matthew 5:38-42) If we were to assume that Jesus is teaching on retaliation and revenge rather than pacifism in verses 38-42, how would you sum up his teaching in a single sentence?
http://www.joyfulheart.com/forums/index.php?showtopic=758

Overcoming Evil with Good

Love can overcome evil, and we Christians are called to overcome evil in this world by love, our own self-giving love as we are breathed upon by God's Holy Spirit.

The Bible carries a number of examples and statements of this principle, both in the Old Testament and the New: The spirit of the law is quite clear.

> "If you come across your enemy's ox or donkey wandering off, be sure to take it back to him. If you see the donkey of someone who hates you fallen down under its load, do not leave it there; be sure you help him with it." (Exodus 23:4-5)

> "Do not seek revenge or bear a grudge against one of your people, but love your neighbor as yourself. I am the Lord." (Leviticus 19:18)

> "If there is a poor man among your brothers in any of the towns of the land that the Lord your God is giving you, do not be hardhearted or tightfisted toward your poor brother. Rather be openhanded and freely lend him whatever he needs." (Deuteronomy 15:7-8)

> "If your enemy is hungry, give him food to eat;

> if he is thirsty, give him water to drink.
> In doing this, you will heap burning coals on his head,
> and the Lord will reward you." (Proverbs 25:21-22)

> "If I have rejoiced at my enemy's misfortune
> or gloated over the trouble that came to him,
> I have not allowed my mouth to sin
> by invoking a curse against his life...." (Job 31:29-30)

> "Do not say, "I'll do to him as he has done to me;
> I'll pay that man back for what he did." (Proverbs 24:29)

> "Do not repay anyone evil for evil. Be careful to do what is right in the eyes of every-
> body.... Do not be overcome by evil, but overcome evil with good" (Romans 12:17, 21).

One of the best examples of loving your enemies we have seen in the twentieth century is the leadership of Dr. Martin Luther King, Jr. in the Civil Rights Movement in the 1950s and 60s. King was stabbed, beaten, jailed, and finally shot for his opposition to white-imposed segregation in the South. Please read my synopsis of his sermon on "Loving Your Enemies" in Excursus 5 to get a flavor of what he believed and lived out.

Christian Pacifism

Some interpret this passage as teaching pacifism. My Presbyterian minister grandfather was a pacifist during World War I. Other ancestors were Quakers, traditionally opposed to war. They would argue, perhaps:

> War is certainly a great evil. How could a Christian ever serve as a soldier? As such you
> would not be "turning the other cheek," but the opposite, taking a human life. You can't
> love your enemies and be a soldier. Peacemakers are the sons of God; soldiers are just
> the opposite of that. War also requires deceiving the enemy, which is antithetical to the
> truth-telling required of a Christian. One can't possibly imagine Jesus fighting in a war.

While I respect the great moral courage shown by many who hold such a position, I respectfully disagree.

Yes, war is a great evil. It has been used throughout the ages as a tool of proud leaders to impose their will on others. There have certainly been unjust wars. I could see myself opposing an unjust war, and perhaps refuse to serve in one. The issues are confused, of course, by human evil. Even "just" wars always seem to involve some injustice and hatred, and usually racism and atrocities. War brings out the worst in some people.

We see in Paul's writings, however, a clearly articulated teaching of civil authorities acting as administrators of justice.

"For rulers hold no terror for those who do right, but for those who do wrong. Do you want to be free from fear of the one in authority? Then do what is right and he will commend you. For he is God's servant to do you good. But if you do wrong, be afraid, for **he does not bear the sword for nothing**. He is God's servant, an agent of wrath to bring punishment on the wrongdoer. Therefore, it is necessary to submit to the authorities, not only because of possible punishment but also because of conscience." (Romans 13:3-5)

This judicial and police function of the state is clearly supported in scripture.

Thus, I contend that absolute pacifism, that is, opposition to any and all wars, is not taught in the Bible. Moreover, there are times when you must clearly defend yourself and defeat evil, if you don't want it to prevail. Hitler murdered millions of Jews, Gypsies, dissenters, and religious leaders because the German people acquiesced to it. A world war to right these wrongs and bring justice to the peoples of the earth was righteous.

People sometimes read pacifism into Jesus' teaching in the Sermon on the Mount by a lack of care regarding the intent and meaning of the passage. As I have indicated above, "an eye for an eye" is God's law to guide judges in administering law fairly and justly. What Jesus is faulting is the Pharisees' misinterpretation of the law that justified their *personal* vengeance and retaliation against their enemies. Be very clear on this:

1. **"An eye for an eye"** applies to justice under law. This is for God to execute. It **does not** apply to any individual's personal action. God delegates part of this role to the state; the remainder he executes on Judgment Day:

    "Do not take revenge, my friends, but leave room for God's wrath, for it is written: 'It is mine to avenge; I will repay,' says the Lord" (Romans 12:19, quoting Deuteronomy 32:35).

2. **"Turn the other cheek"** applies to personal ethics and treatment of our enemies. It **does not** apply to the judicial function of God or of the state.

Sometimes we simultaneously are called upon as citizens here on earth to fulfill a dual role, such as a policeman, soldier, or judge, at the same time as we operate on a personal level according to Jesus' insistence on loving our enemies. For example, it is entirely possible that a victim will forgive an offence while the offender is sentenced by a judge to punishment for his crimes. We must separate the personal from the judicial or we get in trouble. Of course, the judicial function, too, is to be guided by God's laws. It should operate under God, not as a law to itself.

Martin Luther the Reformer put it this way:

"Christ is not tampering with the responsibility and authority of the government, but he is teaching individual Christians how to live personally, apart from their official position and authority.... A Christian should not [use violence to] resist evil; but within the limits of his office, a secular person should oppose firmly every evil."[7]

Q5. (Matthew 5:39-44) If the principle that underlies verses 39-42 is found in verse 44 and 22:39, are there times we must defend ourselves physically against evil men in order to fulfill the principle? What might be some examples?
http://www.joyfulheart.com/forums/index.php?showtopic=759

Be Perfect (5:48)

Our passage concludes with a firm command:

"Be perfect, therefore, as your heavenly Father is perfect." (5:48)

It has become axiomatic to excuse ourselves by saying, "After all, nobody's perfect." It seems self-evident. But too often it becomes a reason not to rise to anything better. Jesus calls us to rise above our imperfect love to his perfect *agape* love.

The word translated "Be perfect" in verse 48 is Greek *teleios*, "complete, perfect," from the verb *teleō*, "bring to an end, finish, complete, carry out, accomplish."[8] Leon Morris comments:

Teleios has the meaning 'having attained the end (*telos*) or aim'; if anything has fully attained that for which it is designed, it is perfect. It can refer to the maturity of an adult man – the end or aim of that to which the boy points."[9]

God's love for the just and the unjust is the end or purpose or goal of our love. It requires us to renounce our selfish and discriminatory love in favor of love for all, even love for our enemies. Christ's death on the cross for our sins is perhaps the best example of all.

"Greater love has no one than this, that he lay down his life for his friends." (John 15:13)

But in a sense, Jesus did even more: He laid down his life for his enemies. The Apostle Paul observes:

"Very rarely will anyone die for a righteous man, though for a good man someone might possibly dare to die. But God demonstrates his own love for us in this: While we were still sinners, Christ died for us." (Romans 5:7-8)

---

[7] Martin Luther, quoted by Graham N. Stanton, "Sermon on the Mount/Plain," DJG, p. 738.
[8] Reinier Schippers, "Goal, *telos*," *International Dictionary of New Testament Theology*, 2:59-66.
[9] Morris, *Matthew*, pp. 133-134, footnote 172.

What the Prince of Peace did was to put to an end the enmity between God and man. The wrath of God for sin was poured out upon him, "and by his stripes we are healed" (Isaiah 53:5).

We Christians cannot settle for a love that only loves friends. Instead we are to embrace a greater love, impossible unless the Holy Spirit grows this love within our hearts. We aspire to a love that forgives the unforgivable, a love that bridges the enmity of decades, a love that refuses to tire from rejection, a love that never gives up. This is the love we are called to. This quality of love is God's perfection and glory, and is to be ours as well.

Will we attain it? Yes, to some degree, though I'm sure we will fall short of its fullness. Aspirations, goals have a way of reformulating what we try for, what we seek, what we strive for, so we are commanded to Be Perfect.

We are not to reinterpret the Law in order to justify our hatreds, as the Pharisees did. Rather, we are to redefine ourselves, be renewed in God's image, and imbued with His Spirit so that we might "be perfect, as our heavenly Father is perfect."

Q6. (Matthew 5:48) In the context, what do you think verse 48 means for the Christian? Is perfection taught here? Does maturity express the idea best? How about the doctrine of "sinless perfection"? How does verse 48 relate to verse 45?
http://www.joyfulheart.com/forums/index.php?showtopic=760

Prayer

Father, we have such a long way to go in our love. Forgive us for our selfishness, our pettiness. Help us to love with constancy – as you do. Teach us to love our enemies – as you do. Teach us to overcome evil with good – as you do. Have mercy upon us as we learn to have mercy on others. In Jesus' name, we pray. Amen.

Excursus 5: Loving Your Enemies Case Study: Dr. Martin Luther King Jr.

One of the best examples in the twentieth century of loving one's enemies, I believe, was Dr. Martin Luther King, Jr.'s leadership of the Civil Rights Movement of the 1950s and 60s. King was not flawless. But he was a great leader, and a great Christian leader, too. In the face of judicial injustice, he led his people to civil disobedience in order to stimulate the conscience of the American people.

At that time, many people, especially in the South, took the relationship between whites and blacks for granted. They were not really cognizant of the terrible injustice towards blacks. I can remember traveling in the South in the early 60s seeing two drinking fountains: one labeled "white," the other "colored." Segregation of the races was the law of the land. Blacks were widely excluded from jobs, restaurants, clubs, schools, churches, etc.

King viewed this as moral injustice and aimed to change it. Instead of calling for violence against the white oppressors, as some black leaders did in the 70s, no inner cities were burned during his watch. Instead he strongly and vigorously taught his followers to love their oppressors and to pray for them. The Civil Rights Movement was a prayer movement as well as a political movement. King and his followers were subjected to brutality, beatings, savage dogs, high pressure hoses but determined to love in spite of what their enemies did to them.

On November 17, 1957 in Dexter Avenue Baptist Church in Montgomery, Alabama, Dr. King gave a sermon entitled "Loving Your Enemies," using as his text Matthew 5:43-45.

He began, "I want to turn your attention to this subject: 'Loving Your Enemies.' It's so basic to me because it is a part of my basic philosophical and theological orientation – the whole idea of love, the whole philosophy of love." First, Dr. King outlined three ways to go about loving your enemies:

1. Look within yourself to realize that you are not perfect, and something you have done might have sparked their hatred,
2. Discover the element of good in your enemy, and
3. When the opportunity presents itself for you to defeat your enemy, that is the time that you must not do it.

Then he considered the reasons why you should love your enemies:

1. Hate only intensifies the existence of hate and evil in the universe,

2. Hate distorts the personality of the hater, and

3. Love has within it a redemptive power.

Finally, King concluded that oppressed people faced three choices:

"One of them is to rise up against their oppressors with physical violence and corroding hatred. But, oh, this isn't the way. For the danger and the weakness of this method is its futility. Violence creates many more social problems than it solves...."

"Another way is to acquiesce and to give in, to resign yourself to the oppression.... But that too isn't the way because non-cooperation with evil is as much a moral obligation as is cooperation with good.

"But there is another way. And that is to organize mass non-violent resistance based on the principle of love. It seems to me that this is the only way as our eyes look to the future. As we look out across the years and across the generations, let us develop and move right here. We must discover the power of love, the power, the redemptive power of love. And when we discover that we will be able to make of this old world a new world. We will be able to make men better. Love is the only way. Jesus discovered that...."

"There is a little tree planted on a little hill and on that tree hangs the most influential character that ever came in this world. But never feel that that tree is a meaningless drama that took place on the stages of history. Oh no, it is a telescope through which we look out into the long vista of eternity, and see the love of God breaking forth into time. It is an eternal reminder to a power-drunk generation that love is the only way. It is an eternal reminder to a generation depending on nuclear and atomic energy, a generation depending on physical violence, that love is the only creative, redemptive, transforming power in the universe...."

"We will be able to matriculate into the university of eternal life because we had the power to love our enemies, to bless those persons that cursed us, to even decide to be good to those persons who hated us, and we even prayed for those persons who despitefully used us."

Dr. King concluded in prayer:

"Oh God, help us in our lives and in all of our attitudes, to work out this controlling force of love, this controlling power that can solve every problem that we confront in all areas. Oh, we talk about politics; we talk about the problems facing our atomic civilization. Grant that all men will come together and discover that as we solve the crisis and solve these problems – the international problems, the problems of atomic energy, the problems of nuclear energy, and yes, even the race problem – let us join together in a great fellowship of love and bow down at the feet of Jesus. Give us this strong determination. In the name and spirit of this Christ, we pray. Amen."[1]

---

[1] Copyright by Estate of Martin Luther King, Jr., Atlanta, Georgia.

III. Piety in the Kingdom (6:1-18)

In chapter 6 of Matthew we reach a shift of topics. In chapter 5, Jesus has given a small, paradoxical picture in the Beatitudes of the believer's character, and pointed out his call to believers to be salt and light in the world. Next, he has explained the relationship of his teaching to the Law, to renew the inherent spirit of that Law in distinction to the Pharisees who have dealt so much with the externals that sometimes they have missed the point entirely. Now he turns to the nature of true piety, which had also become distorted in the Judaism of Jesus' day.

We'll consider this section in two chapters:

7. Giving, Prayer and Fasting (6:1-8, 16-18)
8. The Lord's Prayer (6:9-15)

Titian, "St. John the Alms-Giver" (1545-50), oil on canvas, St. Giovanni Elemosinario, Venice.

7. Giving, Prayer, and Fasting (6:1-8, 16-18)

In chapter 6, Jesus turns toward true piety. To understand this, first we need to understand the deep sense of duty towards the poor that infused Judaism. The Law provided that one should not harvest a field completely, but let the corners go unharvested and leave behind enough stalks for the poor to glean after them (Leviticus 19:9; 23:22). Ruth and Naomi, for example, were widows able to survive by this means.

The poorest of the poor, like Ruth in the Bible, would glean in a field after the harvesters had finished in order to gather enough food for the day. Jean François Millet (1814-1875), "The Gleaners" (1857), 84x111 cm, Musée d'Orsay, Paris..

Moreover, kindness to the poor was considered a religious duty.

"He who despises his neighbor sins,
but blessed is he who is kind to the needy." (Proverbs 14:20-21)

"He who oppresses the poor shows contempt for their Maker,
but whoever is kind to the needy honors God." (Proverbs 14:31)

"He who is kind to the poor lends to the Lord,
and he will reward him for what he has done." (Proverbs 19:17)

The scriptures refer to God as the defender of the widow and the fatherless (Psalm 72:12-14). Those, then who know God will do as he does (Jeremiah 22:16). In the parable of the Sheep and the Goats, Jesus talks about eternal judgment having to do with how the poor were treated (Matthew 25:42, 45). See Excursus 6, which follows for a more comprehensive listing of "Verses on How God Looks at the Poor."

According to Harvard scholar George Foot Moore, caring for the poor was considered an important duty. If one had it in his power, one should give enough to meet the poor person's actual need. Sometimes to help the poor man save face, the money might be given as a loan, thus Jesus' statement, "Give to the one who asks you, and do not turn away from the one who wants to borrow from you" (Matthew 5:42). A man's first obligation was to support the dependent members of his own family, then to relieve the necessities of his relatives and those in his town.

However, giving alms to the poor was not just personal and direct. By the end of the first century AD, many Jewish communities had organized a community chest to care for the poor. In each town two collectors were appointed to make their rounds of the townspeople each Friday to take up the weekly collection for the poor in money or in goods. Then three others were appointed to give out to the poor every Friday enough to provide for the coming week.[1]

As corrupt, misguided, and inefficient as our modern-day welfare systems may be, they are grounded on a righteous and godly foundation of caring for the poor. However a given community chooses to care for the poor, the duty to do so is from God. Whether this responsibility is carried on by churches, or charitable institutions, or by the government, or by a combination of these is not dictated by scripture so much as prudence. We all desire to provide for actual need without perpetuating the need for charity to continue forever after.

Attitudes Toward the Poor

"So when you give to the needy..." Jesus says. Notice that he took for granted that we *would* give to the needy. What he was concerned about was the motive and attitude with which the alms were given. Without real love, there would be no reward.

I am concerned about a general attitude that many Christians have toward the poor.

First, I sense a **superior attitude**. We often assume that it's their own fault that people are poor. Of course, in some cases this is true. Laziness and irresponsibility, gambling, alcohol, and drugs have each taken a tremendous toll. But sometimes trauma in Vietnam, Iraq, or elsewhere has preceded a life of addiction and escape. Many, many of the poor are poor because of circumstances fully or partially beyond their control. Divorce has decimated families, those fragile units upon which our society depends. After divorce in America, the man typically increases his standard of living. But divorce often consigns to poverty the wife and children. Many of the poor come from broken families that have not instilled in them the discipline and training necessary to get and retain a job. Sickness and injury and mental illness bring many to poverty. Layoffs and

---

[1] George Foot Moore, *Judaism in the First Centuries of the Christian Era: The Age of Tannaim* (1927-30; reprinted by Hendrickson, 1997), vol. 2, chapter 7.

shifting of labor to lower cost overseas workers cripple others.

Yet, somehow we feel superior. We must learn to see the poor as our brothers and our sisters. Jesus told us to consider the poor as himself. He said that how we care for the poor and suffering is how we care for him (Matthew 25:31-46). May God convict us of our superior attitudes. There may well be times in our lives when we ourselves have been or will be poor. Love and a sense of brotherhood with the poor are what Jesus calls us to.

Second, this superior attitude can lead to **resentment**. We justly resent the widespread abuse of the welfare system. There are many wrongs we need to right. Political conservatives sometimes struggle with the growth of what they consider "big government" and a "welfare state." No matter what our political bent, we must guard ourselves so that our political resentment does not extend to the poor themselves.

Third, our resentment may come from **greed**. None of us wants to pay so much in taxes. And if somehow welfare were localized and separated from our general taxes, we might be able to give more personally with a purer heart. But let's not allow greed to turn us away from our Christian obligation to care for the poor among us.

The Root of Pride (6:1)

As Jesus begins to discuss expressions of piety in his day, he zeros in on the chief problem with spiritual life: its constant tendency to go to our head and turn into a hollow religiosity.

> "Be careful not to do your 'acts of righteousness' before men, to be seen by them. If you do, you will have no reward from your Father in heaven." (6:1)

The word translated "Be careful" (NIV), "beware" (NRSV), or "take heed" (KJV) is Greek *prosechō*, which means "to turn toward," specifically in this context, "to be in a state of alert, be concerned about, care for, take care."[2] It serves to highlight the command which follows it.

The next phrase is, "To be seen by them." How much of our lives are lived to "be seen by them." We stretch to "keep up with the Joneses." We dress to impress and attract and entice. We speak to manipulate and ingratiate and seek our own advancement. We work very hard to create an impression to the outside world. But we are critical of the Pharisees who sometimes did the same thing.

---

[2] *Prosechō*, BDAG 879-880, 1.

The Audience of One (6:3-4)

When I heard Bill Hybels, pastor of Willow Creek Community Church near Chicago, speak some time ago, I was impressed with his passion to "live for the audience of One." So much of our time is spent trying to advance ourselves or impress others. How about God?

Jesus pointed out to his disciples the widow who gave two small copper coins, and gave more than the all the rich people combined (Mark 12:41-42). She gave all she had, but she gave for "the Audience of One" and he was indeed watching.

One day Jesus told a parable to underscore this point:

> "Two men went up to the temple to pray, one a Pharisee and the other a tax collector.

James J. Tissot, The Widow's Mite (1896-1904), watercolor, Brooklyn Museum, New York

> The Pharisee stood up and prayed about himself: 'God, I thank you that I am not like other men–robbers, evildoers, adulterers–or even like this tax collector. I fast twice a week and give a tenth of all I get.'
>
> But the tax collector stood at a distance. He would not even look up to heaven, but beat his breast and said, 'God, have mercy on me, a sinner.'
>
> I tell you that this man, rather than the other, went home justified before God. For everyone who exalts himself will be humbled, and he who humbles himself will be exalted." (Luke 18:10-14)

The Pharisee prayed in his pride, but the tax collector prayed in his humility, and was heard by "The Audience of One."

As Christians, our lives are to be lived hour by hour, day by day for our Lord. When we give, we are to give out of love for the Lord. When we pray, out of devotion to him. When we fast, out of a passion to draw closer to him. That is surely the spirit of this passage.

> "But when you give to the needy, do not let your left hand know what your right hand is doing, so that your giving may be in secret. Then your Father, who sees what is done in secret, will reward you." (6:3-4)

We aren't to give to impress others, but for "the audience of One." It matters to God that we don't burn out our spiritual devotion in impressing others. It matters very much to him. He wants us to live in devotion for him alone. He wants us to have a pure heart, a single heart.

Trumpeting Our Piety (6:2-3)

How different is a religion that makes a show of piety. In Jesus' day some of the Pharisees would give alms with great show "to be honored by men." We know by reading the rabbinical writings of Judaism that this was not the heart of Pharisaism. It was an aberration. But hypocrisy exists in any day.

It can exist in our day, too. I am appalled at some of the fundraising methods used in the name of Christ with little consideration to Biblical teaching:

- Putting a person's name on a publicly displayed plaque if they give at a certain level.
- Getting people to publicly wave a certain denomination of bill that they plan to give.
- Trooping down to the front of the church to make an offering that can be seen by all.

I'm sure you could name other travesties of this kind. Anything that appeals to a person's temptation to exalt himself or herself is a poor motivation for Christian giving.

Pride, the Universal Temptation

The root problem, really, is the need for love. Pride has a way of waving and gesturing: "Hey, look at me. I need your attention. I need your approval." Pride really comes from an internal weakness and insecurity, an unmet need for love.

As I look at my own weaknesses, this is one. What I am learning is that God wants to fill my need for love and acceptance with his own love, flooding me with love and acceptance at the very core of my being. Where I clamor to receive love from everyone else, I really need to get away with God – in secret – and commune with him, and so receive this assurance and love portion that I need.

Isn't it interesting that the cure for public pride is secret time with the Father? If we will give to him in secret, he will also give to us in secret an unbounded blessing, so that we are free to give to others without needing to receive praise or even thanks in exchange.

And as he cures the root, he also desires to cure the branch. He tells us to love God with all our heart, and love our neighbor as ourselves. Instead of looking within to satisfy our own selves, the cure is to look outward to God and others, and give to them in love.

Love, finally, is the answer. Receiving God's love fully and lavishly, and then reflecting and returning it to others – that is the life lived in love.

Purely. Simply. Secretly.

That is how we are to do our "acts of righteousness."

Q1. (Matthew 6:1-18) How do the commands in this section relate to "performing for the audience of One"? What is the antidote for the chief sin that is addressed here? In what ways do churches and non-profit organizations use this sin to motivate people to give?
http://www.joyfulheart.com/forums/index.php?showtopic=761

Q2. (Matthew 5:42 and 6:1-4) How does Jesus' teaching here and in 5:42 on giving to the needy influence you and your attitudes towards the poor? What will you do differently as a result? What keeps us from giving more to the poor? Is that a good enough reason?
http://www.joyfulheart.com/forums/index.php?showtopic=762

Secret Prayer (6:5-6)

At the beginning of this part of the Sermon on the Mount, Jesus stated the principle:

> "Be careful not to do your 'acts of righteousness' before men, to be seen by them. If you do, you will have no reward from your Father in heaven" (6:1)

The first example of this was in the way we give to those in need. The second relates to how, where, and why we pray, and a third to how we are to fast.

> "And when you pray, do not be like the hypocrites, for they love to pray standing in the synagogues and on the street corners to be seen by men. I tell you the truth, they have received their reward in full." (Matthew 6:5)

In Jesus' day some religious people, probably of the Pharisee party, took great pride in their devotion, and prayed in public so that people could see how spiritual they were, "to be seen by men."

Jesus isn't against public prayer. Jesus himself often prayed in public. But he argues that praying in public *in order to* be thought by others to be pious is offensive. The reward for such self-seeking prayers is merely the applause of men. Any reward from God is forfeit. Instead, Jesus tells his disciples,

> "But when you pray, go into your room, close the door and pray to your Father, who is unseen. Then your Father, who sees what is done in secret, will reward you." (6:6)

The King James Version translates the phrase as, "enter into thy closet," making children sometimes feel holy when they pray among their hanging clothing. The Greek word is *tameion*, which means, "storeroom," then generally, a room in the interior of a house, "inner room."[3]

The point here is secrecy. We are not just to retire into a private place, but also to close the door, so that we won't be tempted to impress anyone by our piety. Surely God can hear our prayers in crowded places and wide open fields, but to deal with religious pride that was so prevalent in his day (and in ours), Jesus stressed the privacy of prayer.

Someone said that character is doing the same thing whether anyone is watching or not. That is a good barometer for our prayer life, too.

As I have worked to develop disciples for Jesus, I have found one

Alexandre Bida (French painter, 1823-1895), "The Prayer in Secret," engraving, in Edward Eggleston, *Christ in Art* (New York: Fords, Howard, & Hulbert, 1874).

consistent element that either severely retards or greatly accelerates growth – private devotions: prayer, meditation, Bible reading, and the like. Those who set aside time alone with God grow. Those who don't, stagnate.

So perhaps Jesus isn't just dealing with pride here. He is offering a practical suggestion about prayer in general. Pray in private for God's benefit as an act of discipleship.

---

[3] *Tameion*, BDAG 988, 2.

Prayer in Few Words (6:7)

Unlike Jesus' examples of giving alms (6:2-4) and fasting (6:16-18), Jesus amplifies his teaching on prayer. He says,

> "And when you pray, do not keep on babbling like pagans, for they think they will be heard because of their many words. Do not be like them, for your Father knows what you need before you ask him." (6:7-8)

This raises two questions. First, what kind of babbling is he referring to? The Greek word is *polylogia*, which means "speech of tedious length, much speaking, wordiness, long-windedness."[4] The King James rendering "use not vain repetitions" is a bit misleading, since the Greek word implies neither "vain" nor "repetitious." In fact, Jesus himself repeated the same prayer three times in the Garden of Gethsemane (Matthew 26:44).

Rather, Jesus is saying, don't think that eloquence or wordiness are necessary to communicate with God. So many times people are hesitant to offer a prayer in public because, they say, "I don't know the right words to use in prayer." I think that by example we (myself included) have taught people that prayer must be fluent and use the proper religious language. Many people feel that if they can't pray that way, they don't know how to pray at all.

Perhaps the best comparative example of prayer in the Bible was the Pharisee and the tax collector that was quoted above (Luke 18:10-14). The Pharisee prayed 33 words compared to the tax collector's seven. But God heard the shorter prayer because it was offered to Him sincerely rather than out of pride.

Q3. (Matthew 6:5-7) Why does Jesus tell us to pray in secret? Though public prayer in church gatherings is commanded in scripture (Acts 1:14; 2:42; 1 Timothy 2:1), in which circumstances might public prayer in a church service be contrary to the spirit of Jesus' instructions in these verses? How do flowery prayers hinder the development of disciples?
http://www.joyfulheart.com/forums/index.php?showtopic=763

Why Pray at All? (6:8)

One phrase in Jesus' teaching is especially troubling:

---

[4] *Polylogia*, BDAG 847.

"... For your Father knows what you need before you ask him" (6:8b).

It raises a very important question: Why should we pray at all? If God knows our need before we ask him, then he knows what we will say to him when we pray. So why bother? Why go to the trouble of formulating our prayer into words before God?

One popular answer is that we pray more for our own benefit than God's. Not only does it fit with a popular psychological view of the devotional life in our own day, it is undergirded with support from some of the great Protestant theologians. John Calvin said:

> "Believers do not pray with the view of informing God about things unknown to him, or of exciting him to do his duty, or of urging him as though he were reluctant. On the contrary, they pray in order that they may arouse themselves to seek him, that they may exercise their faith in meditating on his promises, that they may relieve themselves from their anxieties by pouring them into his bosom; in a word, that they may declare that from him alone they hope and expect, both for themselves and for others, all good things."[5]

Luther put it more succinctly yet:

> "By our praying ... we are instructing ourselves more than we are him."[6]

I'll agree that prayer is not instructing God. But I strongly believe that prayer is more than self-talk. Prayer is not primarily speaking to hear ourselves talk (no matter how beneficial that may be).

Prayer is communicating with God. It is not "thinking good thoughts" as some people put it when they say, "Hold a good thought for me," as if the positive power of good thoughts is the essence of prayer.

Prayer is communicating with God. It is speaking to him. It is formulating our thoughts to him. And, more important yet, it is engaging him in conversation. Jesus wants us to learn to communicate with God. And so he teaches his disciples a model prayer, The Lord's Prayer (6:9-15), which we'll consider in detail in the next chapter.

Q4. (Matthew 6:8) If God knows what you need before you ask him, why should you ask him at all? What sense does prayer really make? Are we mainly to talk for our own edification and encouragement? Why or why not?
http://www.joyfulheart.com/forums/index.php?showtopic=764

---

[5] John Calvin, *Commentary on a Harmony of the Evangelists* (1558), quoted by Stott, *The Message of the Sermon on the Mount*, p. 145.
[6] Quote by Stott, *Message*, p. 145.

Fasting (6:16-18)

> "¹⁶ When you fast, do not look somber as the hypocrites do, for they disfigure their faces to show men they are fasting. I tell you the truth, they have received their reward in full. ¹⁷ But when you fast, put oil on your head and wash your face, ¹⁸ so that it will not be obvious to men that you are fasting, but only to your Father, who is unseen; and your Father, who sees what is done in secret, will reward you." (Matthew 6:16-18)

Jesus concludes his discussion of piety for God's eyes only with a section on fasting. We are not to make sure that people see us suffering and think of how pious we are. Rather, we are to face the world groomed so that our fasting will not be obvious. Fasting is to God, not to men.

Note that Jesus doesn't say, "If you fast..." but "When you fast...." Though he and his disciples didn't practice fasting as a discipline of their band (9:14-15), Jesus himself fasted in preparation for his ministry (4:2) and he implied that Christian disciples would fast following his time of earthly ministry (9:15).

While this is not the place for a thorough discussion of fasting, it is important to determine *why* we are fasting. It is not to go on a hunger strike to force God to do something. That is foolish. Nor is the purpose of a Biblical fast to go on a diet or lose weight or purify one's system. Fasting is to purify the believer's heart, to spend time focusing on God, to learn to deny the physical in order to grow the spiritual. Fasting is for repentance, for sorrow, for purification. Fasting helps us become more sensitive to God. Fasting is a discipline designed to help us draw closer to God.

In all our deeds of righteousness and piety – and we should expect to find these in the sincere believer – we are to be careful to do these for the proper motive, for the Audience of One, not for the acclaim of others. Worship is for God, and for him alone.

Prayer

Father, so often we do religious acts for others' benefit. Forgive us! Let our prayers and giving and worship be for you, and you alone. We seek to please you, our Father. That is our heart. In Jesus' name, and in conformity with his teachings, we pray. Amen.

Excursus 6. Verses on How God Looks at the Poor

All verses are given in the NIV translation.

"Do not pervert justice; do not show partiality to the poor or favoritism to the great, but judge your neighbor fairly." (Leviticus 19:15)

"The LORD sends poverty and wealth; he humbles and he exalts." (1 Samuel 2:7)

"But you, O God, do see trouble and grief; you consider it to take it in hand. The victim commits himself to you; you are the helper of the fatherless. " (Psalm 10:14)

"'Because of the oppression of the weak and the groaning of the needy, I will now arise,' says the LORD. 'I will protect them from those who malign them.'" (Psalm 12:5)

"My whole being will exclaim, 'Who is like you, O LORD? You rescue the poor from those too strong for them, the poor and needy from those who rob them." (Psalm 35:10)

"For he will deliver the needy who cry out, the afflicted who have no one to help. He will take pity on the weak and the needy and save the needy from death. He will rescue them from oppression and violence, for precious is their blood in his sight." (Psalm 72:12-14)

"Defend the cause of the weak and fatherless; maintain the rights of the poor and oppressed. Rescue the weak and needy; deliver them from the hand of the wicked." (Psalm 82:3-4)

"He satisfies the thirsty and fills the hungry with good things." (Psalm 107:9)

"I know that the LORD secures justice for the poor and upholds the cause of the needy." (Psalm 140:12)

"He upholds the cause of the oppressed and gives food to the hungry. The LORD sets prisoners free." (Psalm 146:7)

"A poor man's field may produce abundant food, but injustice sweeps it away." (Proverbs 13:23)

"The poor are shunned even by their neighbors, but the rich have many friends. He who despises his neighbor sins, but blessed is he who is kind to the needy." (Proverbs 14:20-21)

"He who oppresses the poor shows contempt for their Maker, but whoever is kind to the needy honors God." (Proverbs 14:31)

"He who is kind to the poor lends to the Lord, and he will reward him for what he has done." (Proverbs 19:17)

"What a man desires is unfailing love; better to be poor than a liar." (Proverbs 19:22)

"If a man shuts his ears to the cry of the poor, he too will cry out and not be answered." (Proverbs 21:13)

"Rich and poor have this in common:
The LORD is the Maker of them all."
(Proverbs 22:2)

"A generous man will himself be blessed,
for he shares his food with the poor."
(Proverbs 22:9)

"Drunkards and gluttons become poor,
and drowsiness clothes them in rags."
(Proverbs 23:21)

"He who works his land
    will have abundant food,
but the one who chases fantasies
    will have his fill of poverty." (Proverbs 28:19)

"If you see the poor oppressed in a district, and justice and rights denied, do not be surprised at such things; for one official is eyed by a higher one, and over them both are others higher still." (Ecclesiastes 5:8)

"With righteousness he will judge the needy,
with justice he will give decisions
    for the poor of the earth.
He will strike the earth
    with the rod of his mouth;
with the breath of his lips
    he will slay the wicked." (Isaiah 11:4)

"He defended the cause of the poor and needy,
and so all went well.
'Is that not what it means to know me?'
declares the LORD." (Jeremiah 22:16)

"Now this was the sin of your sister Sodom: She and her daughters were arrogant, overfed and unconcerned; they did not help the poor and needy." (Ezekiel 16:49)

"For I was hungry and you gave me nothing to eat, I was thirsty and you gave me nothing to drink ... He will reply, 'I tell you the truth, whatever you did not do for one of the least of these, you did not do for me.'"
(Matthew 25:42, 45)

"Calling his disciples to him, Jesus said, 'I tell you the truth, this poor widow has put more into the treasury than all the others. They all gave out of their wealth; but she, out of her poverty, put in everything – all she had to live on.'" (Mark 12:43-44)

"The poor you will always have with you, and you can help them any time you want. But you will not always have me." (Mark 14:7)

"The Spirit of the Lord is on me,
because he has anointed me
to preach good news to the poor.
He has sent me to proclaim freedom
    for the prisoners
and recovery of sight for the blind,
to release the oppressed...." (Luke 4:18)

"Listen, my dear brothers: Has not God chosen those who are poor in the eyes of the world to be rich in faith and to inherit the kingdom he promised those who love him?" (James 2:5)

8. The Lord's Prayer (6:9-15)

Nowhere does the Bible call Jesus' prayer "The Lord's Prayer," nor is it called the "Our Father." How are we to understand at it? Is it

1. An example prayer?
2. A pattern prayer? or
3. A prayer book prayer to be repeated?

It appears, from the context, to be a pattern prayer. Jesus has just criticized some of the abuses of prayer prevalent in his time. Verses 5-6: Prayer for effect (perhaps typified by the prayer of the righteous Pharisee contrasted by the tax collector's "Be merciful" prayer). Verse 7: Jesus has also contrasted righteous prayer with wordy prayers. He seems to be showing his disciples how to pray properly, avoiding some of the pitfalls, and including an appropriate mix of praise and petition.

James J. Tissot, "The Lord's Prayer" (1896), watercolor, Brooklyn Museum, New York.

Was this the only prayer the disciples were to pray? No. We have many prayers recorded by Jesus, his disciples, and the Apostle Paul. None of them has a word for word correspondence with The Lord's Prayer, but all of them follow patterns Jesus taught in this prayer.

Salutation (6:9)

The prayer begins by addressing God as "Our Father". Bible scholars pretty much agree that behind the Greek word *patēr*, "father", is the word `abba in Jesus' native Aramaic tongue.[1] Rather than the formal word for "father," `abba is the family word, something like the affectionate "Dad" or "Daddy" that we use in English. (See also Mark 14:36; Romans 8:15; Galatians 4:6). There is a formal word for "father," but the word apparently used here stresses the intimate family relationship. This is striking. Jesus was

[1] Gotlob Schrenk, "*pater, ktl.*," TDNT 5:984-985.

teaching his disciples to understand God as their Father. Though the rabbis spoke of God as the Father of the people, Jesus is teaching them to address God as their own personal Father, a new and wonderful revelation.

When you meditate on this a moment, the awe and wonder of it begins to break over you. The God who created the universe is our Father. The God who revealed himself in fire and smoke and thick clouds is our Father. "Father" is a relationship word, and to consider that we have the relationship of child to father with God himself is an awesome thought.

In Jesus' day, "father" included the concepts of care, love, responsibility, discipline, hopes and dreams for one's children, respect, authority, and blessing. In the West, fathers have nowhere near the life-long patriarchal authority that fathers have in the Middle East and Far East. Our fatherhood is but a shell of the powerful concept of "father" that Jesus communicated through this intimate word. Something of the Middle Eastern father is depicted in Jesus' parable of the Father and the Prodigal Son to illustrate the loving, searching, longing quality of our Heavenly Father (Luke 15:11-32).

Some in our generation have excised the word "Father" from their prayers on the basis that too many bad fathers have hurt too many children, and the image of father makes it hard for some to want to come to God. Resist this teaching that contradicts the express teaching and example of Jesus. As you meditate this week on the Lord's Prayer, I encourage you to reclaim for yourself the term "Father." Seek to find out in what ways he is a Father to you.

Notice that Jesus teaches us to call out to God as "our Father." Not just a self-focused "my father," but a communal "our Father." The Lord's Prayer is intended to be prayed not only privately, but especially in the community of God's people, the Church.

Who Art in Heaven (6:9)

Jesus then teaches us to pray to God "who art in heaven," which adds infinity to our understanding of God. Though Solomon built a temple for God, he prayed, "But will God really dwell on earth? The heavens, even the highest heaven, cannot contain you. How much less this temple I have built!" (1 Kings 8:27) Yes, God is greater than his creation, but "the heavens" is a way to understand the greatness of God's dwelling. And when we reflect on God's greatness, it is easier to have faith to ask of him things that seem difficult to us.

Petition 1: That His Name Be Reverenced (6:9c)

The first petition is "hallowed be Thy name." The Greek word is *hagiazō*, which means "to treat as holy, reverence."[2] Our word "Halloween" is short for "All Hallows Eve," or "All Saints' Eve"). "Hallowed" comes from the English word "holy." Why does Jesus include the concept of "hallowed" in the "stripped down" version of his prayer? Because without it, our understanding of "Father" can be distorted.

Our understanding of "Father" could become sentimental to the point of presuming upon and taking advantage of the Father's graciousness towards us. "Hallowed" reminds us that the Father is holy, set apart from sin. That he can be both the Father of sinners and set apart from sin requires Jesus' atonement to reconcile. When we pray, though we pray with the privilege of intimacy to our "Abba, Daddy," we are never to imagine that we are buddies with God, or his equals. He is always our Father, and he is holy and exalted. Jesus teaches us to call God our Father, recognize his exalted place of dwelling, and to reverence him.

The phrase "hallowed be Thy name" may seem a little awkward to us, but in the Near East the idea of "name" stood for the person, his authority, his character, and his activity. When Jesus tells us that the Father's "name" is holy, he means that the Father's whole Person is holy. "Name" can be used as a substitute for a person himself. To paraphrase, "Father, hallowed be your name," means, "Father, may you be treated with the respect and honor that your holiness demands."

It is common for Christians, particularly Christians who come to faith later in their lives, to have a rather profane vocabulary. They may be in the habit of using God's name often, and sometimes almost as a swearword. If, when being surprised, we say "Lord!" or "Christ!" or "Jesus!" or "God!" we are using God's holy name in a profane and common way. We are not reverencing his name, but debasing it. Disciples discipline their mouths and their hearts to reverence the Father's name.

Including "hallowed be your name" in our prayers means that we are to approach the Father, not only with familiarity, but also with reverence and respect for his greatness and holiness. He is our "Dad," but he is also Holy. And as we are learning to pray, we must not forget this.

Q1. (Matthew 6:9) What about our lives and words "hallows" the name of our Father? What desecrates and besmirches it? How should we "hallow" the Father when we begin to pray?
http://www.joyfulheart.com/forums/index.php?showtopic=765

---

[2] *Hagiazō*, BDAG 9-10.

Petitions 2 and 3: For His Kingdom and Will (6:10)

"... Your kingdom come, your will be done on earth as it is in heaven." (6:10)

When we pray, too often we want to get on quickly to our own concerns. But in Jesus' model prayer, we first pray about the concerns of God's Kingdom and his will. This is not the petitioner's prayer so much as the disciple's prayer. This is how disciples are to learn to think and pray and act, with God's Kingdom foremost and predominant in their minds.

"Thy kingdom come...." What are we asking? We can't take this phrase or fragment without looking at the rest of the sentence, since the meaning is found in the context.

"Thy kingdom come, Thy will be done on earth as it is in heaven."

The Kingdom of God

The idea of the Kingdom of God is complex. It goes far back into the Old Testament, at least to the book of Exodus, where God reveals himself as Israel's King. He makes a covenant with them in the form of an ancient suzerain-vassal treaty, a treaty made between a great king and a subservient people (Exodus 19:3-6). The tabernacle in the wilderness is the throne room of a desert monarch. He leads them by day and night. Having no king but Yahweh is one of the unique marks of the Israelites, to the point that their clamoring for a king under Samuel's judgeship is considered a sin (1 Samuel 8).

Saul was Israel's first human king. David, born in Bethlehem, of the tribe of Judah, was the second king and becomes the archetypical king. He is promised that one of his sons will always sit upon the throne (2 Samuel 7), fulfilled ultimately in Jesus Christ. (See above, "Excursus 1. What is the Kingdom of Heaven?")

John comes proclaiming, "Repent, for the kingdom of heaven is near" (Matthew 3:2), and Jesus takes up the same message (Matthew 4:17). He sends out his disciples with the authority to do miracles and proclaim to villages, "The kingdom of God is near you" (Luke 10:9, 11). The kingdom of God comes when Jesus proclaims God's reign, and demonstrates that reign by preaching good news to the poor, freedom for the prisoners, sight for the blind, release for the oppressed, and the Jubilee Day of the Lord (Luke 4:18-19). The kingdom is here in Jesus and his disciples – and in you and me – but it will come fully and completely when Jesus returns to earth to reign over all as King and Lord (Revelation 11:15).

May Your Kingdom Come

Jesus asks us to pray that the Kingdom of God come soon. As one of the last phrases of the Book of Revelation says, "Amen. Come, Lord Jesus" (Revelation 22:20). The

Kingdom will only be present fully when Christ returns, when "The kingdom of the world has become the kingdom of our Lord and of his Christ, and he will reign for ever and ever" (Revelation 11:15).

When we pray, "Your kingdom come," we are asking God to manifest the power and glory of his kingdom in us, and throughout our world. What a prayer! We are praying that Christ might reign over all. We are also asking the Father to hasten the return of Jesus Christ to this earth. Amen!

May Your Will Be Done on Earth

This petition is also a condition for prayer, that all our prayers conform first to God's will. How can we pray the kind of prayer that Jesus wants of us, and still ask for our petty desires, which are so clearly contrary to God's revealed will in the Bible? Teach us to pray, Jesus, we say. Part of that teaching, surely, is to determine God's will and pray along those lines. Prayer for disciples is not to be selfish prayer, but prayer in tune with and guided by God's will.

Q2. (Matthew 6:10) In what sense are we asking that the Father's kingdom should come? Why are we asking for the Father's will to be done here on earth? How should this prayer affect our living?
http://www.joyfulheart.com/forums/index.php?showtopic=766

Petition 4: For Daily Needs (6:11)

The fourth petition in this prayer is for our own needs: "Give us this day our daily bread." This is a curious phrase, because in one short sentence it includes two words that are specific to the current day.

The word translated "This day" is Greek *semēron*, a fairly common word that means "today". But also in the sentence is an extremely rare word, which is usually translated "daily," the word *epiousios*. While its exact derivation is a matter that scholars love to debate, it probably means either "for today" or "for tomorrow."[3] Whichever it means, it is a prayer for the immediate and not distant future.

Bread, of course, is the staple of life. The word is often used for food generally, since bread is the most important food, and is extended here to mean, all of our needs, all those things that we need to sustain us.

---

[3]*Epiousios,* BDAG 376-377.

Receiving from God

So, the prayer means something like, "Give us today what we need for today," and fits very well with Jesus' teaching later in the chapter, "Therefore do not worry about tomorrow, for tomorrow will worry about itself. Each day has enough trouble of its own" (6:34).

The implication here is that we are to come to God with our daily needs. When we say "Give us," that doesn't mean we don't expect to work for our living, but that we recognize God as our Provider. So often in the Western world we have a regular salary that comes like clockwork, month after month, and we take our livelihood for granted. Only when we are laid off or touched by serious illness do we begin to ask daily for his provision. Jesus teaches us to learn to become dependent upon our Father, and to bring to him our daily needs – though we disciples are to put our own needs after the Father's holiness and kingdom and will.

Our Strong Desire for Independence

It's strange, but we long to break free from the necessity of praying this prayer. We would like to store up enough money so that we don't have to worry – or pray – about where our next meal will come from. We would like to be "comfortably" well off, if not rich. We don't want to have to pray for our next meal.

I don't think that Jesus wants us poverty-stricken (though that may happen to us and in that he will be fully able to meet our needs). But he *does* want us to get in the habit of relying upon the Father – for everything. Should we thank God for our food if we have earned the money for it by our own labor? Of course!

> "You may say to yourself, 'My power and the strength of my hands have produced this wealth for me.' But remember the LORD your God, for it is he who gives you the ability to produce wealth, and so confirms his covenant, which he swore to your forefathers, as it is today." (Deuteronomy 8:17-18)

Since it is God who gives us the ability to earn a living, then in a real sense, it is he who "gives" us our daily bread. He strengthens us and provides through us. So often, when we have our health, we take this ability for granted. Jesus is teaching us to look to the Father for every provision.

Sometimes you hear the teaching that we should pray for others' needs, but never for our own, that God will provide without us even asking. Though that teaching sounds pious and faith-filled, it goes directly counter to Jesus' own teaching. We are to ask God for our daily needs. He is interested in our jobs. He cares about your school. He is concerned about the health of your business. He cares about your marriage, and children, and relationships. Your church matters to him.

Jesus teaches us, "Give us today our daily bread." How is it that we so often confuse such a simple concept?

Q3. (Matthew 6:11) Why do we seek to be independent of asking *anyone* for help? Why do we seek to be independent of God? Why should we ask God to "give" us daily bread so long as we can earn a living for ourselves?
http://www.joyfulheart.com/forums/index.php?showtopic=767

Petition 5: Forgiveness (6:12, 14-15)

The fifth petition is for forgiveness. But like the daily-ness of the fourth petition, the fifth petition, too, has a twist. The prayer is:

> "Forgive us our debts,
> as we forgive our debtors."

Three Greek words are used in relationship to sin in the Lord's Prayer in Matthew and Luke. Christians from different traditions use different words as they recite the Lord's Prayer.

"Debt" (Matthew 6:12), Greek *opheilēma*, 1. "debt = what is owed, one's due." 2. In a religious sense debt = sin (as Aramaic *hobah* in rabbinical literature).[4]

"Trespass" (Matthew 6:14-15, KJV), Greek *paraptōma*, "in imagery of one making a false step so as to lose footing: a violation of moral standards, offense, wrongdoing, sin."[5] *Paraptōma* is a compound word from *para-* "beside or near" and *piptō* "to fall." Thayer defines it as "a lapse or deviation from truth and uprightness; a sin, misdeed."[6]

"Sin" (Luke 11:4), Greek *hamartia* "sin. The action itself as well as its result, every departure from the way of righteousness…."[7] Literally, "a failing to hit the mark."[8]

But this prayer, "Forgive us our debts, as we forgive our debtors," is a sort of trick prayer. It is a prayer Jesus uses to teach his disciples the elements of praying aright. The Greek word *hōs*, is a conjunction marking a point of comparison, meaning "as."[9] Jesus

---

[4] *Opheilēma*, BDAG 743.
[5] *Paraptōma*, BDAG 770.
[6] *Paraptōma*, Thayer 485.
[7] *Hamartia*, BDAG 43-44.
[8] *Hamartia*, Thayer 30.
[9] *Hōs*, BDAG 1103-1106.

teaches us to ask God to forgive us "as" we forgive others. In other words, if we forgive others only a little and hold grudges, we are asking God to forgive us only a little and bear a grudge against us. Wow! How many people pray the Lord's Prayer thoughtlessly, and each time they pray, they pray a curse of unforgiveness down upon themselves!

Jesus is making a point in this prayer, a point which he explains in more detail just after the prayer:

> "For if you forgive men when they sin against you, your heavenly Father will also forgive you. But if you do not forgive men their sins, your Father will not forgive your sins." (6:14-15)

How could it be plainer? Jesus had just told his disciples not to seek retribution. "Love your enemies and pray for those who persecute you, that you may be sons of your Father in heaven" (5:44-45). Now he makes it clear that we must forgive, if we are to be considered sons of the Father. Otherwise he will not forgive us.

It is a hard saying, but it is God's way.

Quintessential Forgiveness

Perhaps the most powerful example is that of Jesus himself. "He came to his own [people]," John records, "and his own [people] did not receive him" (John 1:12). His miracles and bread attracted the crowds, but when he had to say some hard things, they would leave as quickly as they had come (John 6:66). A number of times, when he said something they didn't consider Kosher, they tried to kill him, but he slipped away from their grasp (Luke 4:28-30; John 8:59; 10:31). But the time finally came that God had planned (Galatians 4: 4-5). Jesus knew it was coming, and though it filled him with pain to think of it, he faced it openly. This time when his enemies sought to arrest him, he stood forth, said "I am the man," and allowed them to take him. He allowed a mock trial filled with patently false and unsupported charges. He could have called legions of angels to deliver him – the armies of heaven were at his beck and call – but he did not. Soldiers spit in his face and mocked him with a cruel crown of thorns and a purple robe they said made him look like a king. They scourged him nearly to death. Pilate washed his hands and ordered his crucifixion. And as they crucified him, he said, "Father, forgive them, for they know not what they do" (Luke 23:34).

If we are to know and understand God, we must love. We must know and understand forgiveness. If we reject this part of God, we reject the kernel of who he is (1 John 4:16-21). So when Jesus puts it so bluntly in our passage (6:14-15) – you must forgive to be forgiven – we dare not reject this truth.

Isn't this a sort of "works righteousness"? some ask. If you are required to do something before you can be forgiven, then isn't this righteousness by works? No. There's an old story of how to catch a monkey. You chain a cage to a post, and put an orange in the cage. Then when the monkey tries to grasp the orange, and can't pull it through the bars he is trapped. Can't he just release the orange and escape? Yes, but monkeys don't let go of the things that enslave them. They hold on tightly – just like people. And so he is captured, just as surely as if he were in the cage itself.

To be free you must let go of unforgiveness. Is that meritorious so as to earn heaven? No, not any more than repentance from sin is meritorious. We don't earn heaven by repentance or by forgiving. But we must let go of our bondage to sin and hate if we want to receive something better.

The Struggle to Forgive

Forgiveness is sometimes terribly difficult. It's usually not so hard to forgive people we don't know. The people with whom we have a relationship of trust who turn on us, who betray our trust – those people are the hardest to forgive. Husbands, wives, fathers, mothers, children, and boyfriends and girlfriends and our best friends. They can turn on us and wound us deeply. Sometimes we even doubt that "It is better to have loved and lost, than never to have loved at all." Maybe we should withdraw and protect ourselves and never venture out again.

No. The path of health is forgiveness. The path of healing is forgiving.

Sometimes we resist forgiveness because we mistake it for substitutes. In my article "Don't Pay the Price of Counterfeit Forgiveness,"[10] I try to distinguish true forgiveness from its chameleons. True forgiveness does not minimize the sin or the hurt, nor excuse the sinner. True forgiveness chooses not to hold the sin against the sinner any longer. True forgiveness is pardon.

You may be freshly wounded and find your anger too massive to forgive. The injustice may be ongoing, the outrage constant. Perhaps you do not feel you are able to forgive right now. Then I ask you to pray this prayer: "Lord, I find it beyond my ability to forgive this person. I ask you to make me *able* to forgive in the future." Even that prayer may stretch your faith (or obedience) to pray, but pray it anyway. The God of Forgiveness answers prayers like that. He makes a way where there is no way. He takes us beyond ourselves.

Two simple lessons we disciples learn from this petition: (1) we must ask for forgiveness time and time again, and (2) unforgiveness blocks God's blessing.

---

[10] "Don't Pay the Price of Counterfeit Forgiveness," *Moody Monthly,* October 1985, pp. 106-108 (www.joyfulheart.com/maturity/forgive.htm).

Q4. (Matthew 6:12, 14-15) Why should we continually ask forgiveness? How can unforgiveness on our part block God's blessing? How can unforgiveness block God's forgiveness?

http://www.joyfulheart.com/forums/index.php?showtopic=768

Petitions 6 and 7: Help When Tempted (6:13)

> "And lead us not into temptation,
> but deliver us from the evil one." (6:13)

The sixth petition goes beyond asking for forgiveness; it asks for help in our times of trial and temptation so that we do not sin so as to require forgiveness.

Keep Us from Temptation

On its face it is hard to imagine God leading us into temptation at all.

> "When tempted, no one should say, 'God is tempting me.' For God cannot be tempted by evil, nor does he tempt anyone; but each one is tempted when, by his own evil desire, he is dragged away and enticed." (James 1:13-14)

Sometimes we disciples flirt with temptation. We don't exactly seek temptation, but we are attracted to sinful things and so we sort of wink at them. Our resistance is low; we are being "dragged away and enticed" by our "own evil desire," as James puts it. This prayer, "and lead us not into temptation," helps teach us how important it is for us to stop flirting with sin but to actively flee and resist it. That is to be part of the content of our prayers.

Some of you are saying, "But if God knew what I really thought about, or wanted to do, he wouldn't have anything to do with me." Some of you are ashamed of your secret sins, but afraid to open them up to God himself. My dear friends, there is nothing we have done or said or thought that can surprise our Father. The miracle of the cross is that he cares about us in spite of our rebelliousness. This part of the Lord's Prayer reminds us to call upon the Father for strength when we are tempted. We are not to fight a secret war against sin; the Father wants to be our continual partner. He knows your weakness, and mine. And wants to free us and make us whole. What a wonderful Father! What wonderful grace.

But God does *test* us. He allows circumstances that stretch and try us to make us pliable enough that he can remold us into his own image.

> "Consider it pure joy, my brothers, whenever you face trials of many kinds, because you

know that the testing of your faith develops perseverance." (James 1:2-3)

Job was tested. So were Abram and Jacob and Joseph – and Jesus. Trials can be positive, and Jesus wouldn't be teaching us to pray to escape what is strengthening us. So it is probably better to see "Lead us not into temptation," as the negative of its positive counterpart, "but deliver us from evil." Testing may involve temptations, but God's desire is to help us escape temptation – and the tempter. Here we're praying: Don't lead us into places where we can be tempted, but lead us in places where you are, and where we can be free.

Rescue Us from the Evil One

This seventh petition is a prayer for deliverance or rescue from the evil one. It is recognition of the spiritual nature of our warfare against sin. There is not just our own temptation, but a tempter. In our own selves, we are no match for him. So we call out to God for rescue, for deliverance, for salvation from our enemy.

Together, petitions six and seven are asking God: "Keep us from giving into Satan's temptations."

Petition five deals with forgiveness; six and seven with delivering us from sin. Together they make up a prayer that helps us follow Jesus on his path.

A Doxology (6:13c)

"For Thine is the kingdom,
and the power,
and the glory
forever.
Amen."

Having been raised a Protestant, the first time I heard the Catholic version of the Lord's Prayer that left off the last doxology, I was shocked. It was like waiting for the other shoe to drop – and it never did. Actually, the Catholic version may be closer to Jesus' own words than the Protestant version. Let me explain.

The Protestant version of the Lord's Prayer includes a doxology. Our English word "doxology" comes from two Greek words, *doxa* – "praise," and *logos* – "word"; a "word of praise". Sometimes it is called an ascription, since these qualities are "ascribed" to God.

Our best guess is that the doxology was added – perhaps on the basis of 1 Chronicles 29:11-13 – to adapt the Lord's Prayer for liturgical use in the early church.

"[11] Yours, O LORD, is the greatness and the power

and the glory and the majesty and the splendor,

for everything in heaven and earth is yours.

Yours, O LORD, is the kingdom; you are exalted as head over all.

[12] Wealth and honor come from you; you are the ruler of all things.

In your hands are strength and power to exalt and give strength to all.

[13] Now, our God, we give you thanks, and praise your glorious name."

(1 Chronicles 29:11-13)

Although the doxology was probably not part of the original text, Jewish practice was to conclude prayers with a doxology, so it is unlikely that it was offered in New Testament times without some form of doxology.[11] One of my favorite parts of the Lord's Prayer is the doxology. I love to speak out loud as words of declaration and praise, "For Thine is the Kingdom, and the Power, and the Glory," for all these are his in abundance. Praise is a fitting way to conclude our prayer.

The Disciples' Prayer

The Lord's Prayer is deceptively simple. We may pray it often and by rote. We may take its words for granted. But this week – especially this week – let the prayer that Jesus taught his disciples to pray fill your thoughts and meditations. And may its vocabulary become yours.

As we've examined the Lord's Prayer, you can see it isn't a prayer for everyone. It's not for those who hunger for God to rubber-stamp their selfish plans, for it begins with "Thy will be done on earth as it is in heaven." Nor is it for those who feel righteous, for it leads us to ask forgiveness. Nor is it for the vindictive, for it bids us leave our hatred at the altar if we would be forgiven. Nor is it for the self-made man who shuns dependence, for it teaches us to ask God for bread daily. It is a prayer for the obedient disciple

---

[11] The discipline of Textual Criticism tries to determine which version of a disputed text is closest to the original words that Jesus actually said. The original Gospel of Matthew was doubtless copied for use in other churches. And each of those copies became the source of yet more copies, families of copies. In the last century and a half scholars have categorized the earliest manuscripts we have into families of manuscripts according to the similarities found between them. Some of the earliest manuscript families lack the doxology – specifically Alexandrian (Aleph and B), Western (D and most of the Old Latin), and the pre-Caesarean (f^1) types. Those that include it are K L W Delta Theta, Pi, and f^{13}, *et al*. A few manuscripts (such as the *Didache* have a different doxology altogether. Some of the earliest Church Fathers (Tertullian, Origen, and Cyprian, for example) didn't include the doxology in their commentaries on the Lord's Prayer. So W.L. Liefeld, "Lord's Prayer," *ISBE* 3:162. Metzger, *Textual Commentary*, pp. 16-17. At some point the use of the doxology had dropped out in Roman Catholic liturgy. John Calvin (1509-1564) comments, "It is surprising that this clause ... has been left out by the Latins...." (*A Commentary on a Harmony of the Evangelists*, q.v.). John A. Broadas (*Commentary on the Gospel of Matthew* (Judson Press, 1886), p. 139) notes that the doxology wasn't introduced into the English *Book of Common Prayer* until the time of Charles II.

who would know God as he is, in his Fatherhood and glory and holiness. I commend it to you. Pray it thoughtfully and reverently, and let it guide your prayers.

Prayer

Father, teach me to pray the right way, the way Jesus taught us to pray. I confess that my way of praying is often self-centered and self-serving. Teach me to pray. In Jesus' name, I pray. Amen.

IV. Materialism and the Kingdom (6:19-34)

The disciples were just beginning to learn that they could trust God for everything – finances included. In the next section of the Sermon on the Mount, Jesus discusses how to relate to the material world without being consumed by materialism. We'll look at his teaching in two chapters:

9. Temptation to Greed, that is, Idolatry (6:19-24)

10. Temptation to Worry (6:25-34)

David Teniers the Younger (1610-1690), detail of "The Covetous Man" (c. 1648), oil on canvas, National Gallery, London.

9. Temptation to Greed, that is, Idolatry (6:19-24)

In the first part of his teaching in Matthew 6, Jesus talks about true piety towards God: that which seeks its reward in God rather than temporal rewards. It is our purity of heart towards God that he looks at as we worship him. In 6:19-24 he applies this principle of inward purity to the matter of money and storing up treasures (rewards) in heaven.

Storing Up Treasures (6:19-20)

Rembrandt, detail of "The Parable of the Rich Man" (1627), oil on panel, Gemäldegalerie, Berlin.

Verse 19 – "Do not store up for yourselves treasures on earth...." – seems rather abrupt. Though we have no way of knowing for sure, the Sermon on the Mount (which can be read through in about 15 minutes) seems to be a condensed version of Jesus' teaching. In a similar context (just before Jesus' teaching on worry, Luke 12:22-31 || Matthew 6:25-33), Jesus tells the Parable of the Rich Fool in response to a question from the crowd that hinted of greed. Jesus responded:

> "'Watch out! Be on your guard against all kinds of greed; a man's life does not consist in the abundance of his possessions.'

> "And he told them this parable: 'The ground of a certain rich man produced a good crop. He thought to himself, "What shall I do? I have no place to store my crops."

> 'Then he said, "This is what I'll do. I will tear down my barns and build bigger ones, and there I will store all my grain and my goods. And I'll say to myself, 'You have plenty of good things laid up for many years. Take life easy; eat, drink and be merry.'"

'But God said to him, "You fool! This very night your life will be demanded from you. Then who will get what you have prepared for yourself?"

'This is how it will be with anyone who stores up things for himself **but is not rich toward God.**"' (Luke 12:15-21)

I see this parable as the probable missing context of Jesus' similar teaching in the Sermon on the Mount (6:19-24). It contains the same elements of greed and storing up.

Storing up itself is not wrong. Israel was an agrarian culture that took in crops in certain seasons and then stored the grain for use during the rest of the year. An examination of the way the Bible refers to "storing" indicates that normally storing up was considered a positive virtue:

"In the house of the wise are stores of choice food and oil,
but a foolish man devours all he has." (Proverbs 21:20)

"Go to the ant, you sluggard;
consider its ways and be wise!
It has no commander,
no overseer or ruler,
yet it stores its provisions in summer
and gathers its food at harvest." (Proverbs 6:6-8)

Even the Temple had storerooms where the tithe of the people's produce was stored up to be distributed during the year to the priests and Levites whose families depended upon it (Malachi 3:10). Storing up for later use was wise and prudent. Jesus is not commanding against this kind of storing.

In our culture we save for "a rainy day," for times of unemployment. We save to make purchases, to send our children to college, and for retirement. In Israel the elderly could depend upon living with their grown children and being supported that way. In our culture we can't expect that.

Jesus is protesting against the kind of storing up that is a symptom of greed and acquisitiveness, of the love of money, and a love of the independence from God that it seems to allow.

Money is deceptive. If we were to be rich, we imagine that we wouldn't have to be dependent upon the vicissitudes of poor harvests, or working for a living, or having to ask God for our daily bread.

Consider the TV advertising that our state governments use to try to get people to gamble. They appeal to this elusive dream of becoming rich and never having to struggle again. This deceptive greed causes people to invest dollar after dollar in the lottery or other games of chance in pursuit of the dream. The poor, especially, believe the lies that 37 state-run lotteries propagate. In the low-income city of Chelsea, Massachusetts, for example, residents spend 8% of their incomes on lottery tickets.[1]

"You can be the one who wins," the lottery ads tell us, "and you'll never have to worry again."

That's what the Rich Fool believed: "You have plenty of good things laid up for many years. Take life easy; eat, drink and be merry," he told himself. But he was poor towards God (Luke 12:16-20).

Q1. (Luke 12:15-21) Read the Parable of the Rich Fool. What did Jesus condemn him for? Storing his harvest? What is the key verse in this passage? What is the context of this parable? How does this relate to the Sermon on the Mount?
http://www.joyfulheart.com/forums/index.php?showtopic=769

Q2. (Matthew 6:19) Jesus says, "Do not store up for yourselves treasures on earth...." Is he speaking figuratively? Hyperbolically? Generally? Specifically? Is this a new teaching, or an old one?
http://www.joyfulheart.com/forums/index.php?showtopic=770

Treasures in Heaven (6:20)

> "But store up for yourselves treasures in heaven, where moth and rust do not destroy, and where thieves do not break in and steal." (6:20)

So how does one become rich towards God? Just previously, Jesus had taught about doing acts of piety "in secret" so that "your Father, who sees what is done in secret, will reward you" (6:4b). As examples, Jesus spoke of giving alms to the needy, praying in private, and fasting. These acts of love toward God are ways of storing up treasures in heaven (6:20). There's a saying, "You can't take it with you." No, but you can send it on before you, and you do that by your good works with a pure heart for God alone.

I think some Protestants have so absorbed a "saved by grace, not by works" theology (and so we should), that we downplay the concept of rewards in heaven, such as Paul describes in 1 Corinthians 3:8-15, and this final testimony before he was martyred:

---

[1] David M. Halbfinger and Daniel Golden, "The Lottery's Poor Choice of Locations," *Boston Globe*, February 12, 1997, p. A1. Quoted in Dr. James Dobson's April 1999 newsletter on "Gambling's Dirty Little Secrets".

"I have fought the good fight, I have finished the race, I have kept the faith. Now **there is in store** for me the crown of righteousness, which the Lord, the righteous Judge, will **award** to me on that day – and not only to me, but also to all who have longed for his appearing." (2 Timothy 4:7-8)

See the elements of "storing" and "reward" that are in common with Jesus' teaching in our passage?

Q3. (Matthew 6:19-21) According to the Bible, how does one "store up treasures in heaven"? What advantage does this have over accumulating earthly possessions? Why are we uncomfortable with the concept of rewards in heaven?
http://www.joyfulheart.com/forums/index.php?showtopic=771

Your Heart Is the Key to Your Real Treasure (6:21)

Throughout the Sermon on the Mount Jesus returns to the spirit and heart as opposed to the exterior. Here he utters a keen observation.

> "For where your treasure is,
> there your heart will be also." (6:21)

To find out what we *really* love, he says, examine the heart.

Over the years I've married several couples, only to hear later (usually from the wife) that her husband is extremely stingy when it comes to money. It wasn't just frugality, though that's where it may have begun. It is now full-blown loathing to part with money. Who did the husband love more? His wife or his money? I wonder. Sometimes you can tell where a person's real treasure is by examining his heart.

The Window of the Soul (6:22-23)

The next passage is more difficult to understand.

> "[22] The eye is the lamp of the body. If your eyes are good, your whole body will be full of light. [23] But if your eyes are bad, your whole body will be full of darkness. If then the light within you is darkness, how great is that darkness!" (6:22-23)

To us Westerners this seems like a mixed metaphor. The eye to us is an organ of seeing. But to the Israelites it also carried something of the idea of a window, a portal through which light or truth would shine into the mind or soul.

The "good" eye is the eye that sees truth clearly. The "bad" eye is the eye that is deceived by money and greed and power. The tragedy Jesus notes in verse 23b is:

"If then the light within you is darkness, how great is that darkness!" (6:23b)

Many people believe they have it all, only to discover upon coming to Christ that the supposed "light" in them is darkness, that they have been deceived and have nothing at all. The love of money has a way of blinding us to God's truth.

A Tug-of-War Between Two Masters (6:24)

"No one can serve two masters. Either he will hate the one and love the other, or he will be devoted to the one and despise the other. You cannot serve both God and Money." (6:24)

The final verse in this section speaks about the great tug-of-war between the two Masters of our Age (and Jesus' age): God and Mammon. The word "Mammon" (KJV) is transliterated from an Aramaic word. It means "wealth, property."[2] The NIV translates it "Money" – capitalized, since it seems to be personified in verse 25 in contrast with God.

The struggle between God and Money rests chiefly in what we trust in. The Bible says,

Evelyn De Morgan (1855-1919), "The Worship of Mammon" (1909), De Morgan Centre, London.

"If we have food and clothing, we will be content with that. **People who want to get rich fall into temptation and a trap** and into many foolish and harmful desires that plunge men into ruin and destruction. **For the love of money is a root of all kinds of evil**. Some people, eager for money, have wandered from the faith and pierced themselves with many griefs.... Command those who are rich in this present world not to be arrogant nor to **put their hope in wealth**, which is so uncertain, but to put their hope in God, who richly provides us with everything for our enjoyment." (1 Timothy 6:8-10, 17)

"Keep your lives free from the **love of money** and be content with what you have, because God has said, 'Never will I leave you; never will I forsake you.'" (Hebrews 13:5)

---

[2] *Mamōnas*, BDAG 614-615.

When people "put their hope in wealth," they automatically lessen their dependence upon God who has promised to never leave us or forsake us. In a way, Money becomes an alternate point of hope and trust, a substitute God. Jesus put it very boldly:

> "No one can serve two masters. Either he will hate the one and love the other, or he will be devoted to the one and despise the other. You cannot serve both God and Money." (6:24)

The Apostle Paul was very clear. He calls greed or covetousness what it is: idolatry (Colossians 3:5).

Q4. (Matthew 6:24) Jesus seems to make it sound like you can't seek wealth and God simultaneously. Does he really mean this? Is this hyperbole? Figurative? Literal? Can wealthy people serve God in actual fact?
http://www.joyfulheart.com/forums/index.php?showtopic=772

George Frederic Watts (1817-1904), "Mammon" (1884-85), oil on canvas, Tate Collections.

Serving Money

What does it mean to serve Money? I'm sure you've discovered – perhaps the hard way – that "no payments until June of next year" is a seductive way of getting you to purchase what you know you can't afford now. The frequency with which you get bombarded with offers of free credit cards is one indication of what a serious problem people have mortgaging their souls by means of plastic. Of one thing you can be sure: banks don't offer you credit cards in the hope that you'll pay them off every month. They want you to charge them up and then pay them the interest each month.

If you're running the rat race of keeping up with payments on debt, aren't you really serving Money? You serve who owns your time. If you're in debt, perhaps Money owns your time. In 1955, country singer Tennessee Ernie Ford recorded the hit song "Sixteen Tons," written by Merle Travis:

> "You load sixteen tons, what do you get?
> Another day older and deeper in debt.
> Saint Peter don't you call me 'cause I can't go.
> I owe my soul to the company store."[3]

You can either "owe your soul" or determine to get out of a situation where you are doomed to "serve Money." It may take years and some sound financial advisors to get your financial affairs in order and under control again so you can be free to serve God again, but it will be worth it.

The Story of the Rich Young Ruler

One of the saddest stories in the gospels is that of the Rich Young Ruler, who wanted to follow Jesus, but the pull of material things was just too great – and Jesus' demands seemed too much for him:

> "[17] As Jesus started on his way, a man ran up to him and fell on his knees before him. 'Good teacher,' he asked, 'what must I do to inherit eternal life?'
>
> [18] 'Why do you call me good?' Jesus answered. 'No one is good – except God alone. [19] You know the commandments: "Do not murder, do not commit adultery, do not steal, do not give false testimony, do not defraud, honor your father and mother."'
>
> [20] 'Teacher,' he declared, 'all these I have kept since I was a boy.'

Heinrich Hoffman (1824-1911), "Jesus and the Rich Young Man" (1889), Riverside Church, New York.

> [21] Jesus looked at him and loved him. 'One thing you lack,' he said. 'Go, sell everything you have and give to the poor, and you will have **treasure in heaven**. Then come, follow me.' [22] At this the man's face fell. He went away sad, because he had great wealth.
>
> [23] Jesus looked around and said to his disciples, 'How hard it is for the rich to enter the kingdom of God!' [24] The disciples were amazed at his words. But Jesus said again,

---

[3] "Sixteen Tons," written by Merle Travis (©1947, American-Music Inc / Campbell Connelly And Co Ltd.).

'Children, how hard it is to enter the kingdom of God! 25 It is easier for a camel to go through the eye of a needle than for a rich man to enter the kingdom of God.'

26 The disciples were even more amazed, and said to each other, 'Who then can be saved?'

27 Jesus looked at them and said, 'With man this is impossible, but not with God; all things are possible with God.'" (Mark 10:17-27)

Frankly, that's a pretty tough story for rich Westerners to accept. Isn't Jesus just too hard? No. Jesus knows that if a person is that caught up in his own wealth, he can't be a disciple. He can't serve both God and Money. No way!

Where Is Your Heart?

The question, then, becomes, Where is *your* heart? What is *your* real treasure? Has Money become the center of *your* existence? Determine today to put God back squarely in first place. It's where he belongs – and he will help you do just that if you ask him.

Q5. (Matthew 6:21, 24) The love of money can be a pretty subtle thing. Both the rich *and* the poor can love money. Can you describe a time in your life when you were deceived about this, and when the light in you was really darkness? According to Jesus, could desire for money damn a person (Luke 12:15-21)?
http://www.joyfulheart.com/forums/index.php?showtopic=773

Prayer

Father, it's so difficult to really know our own hearts. We can deceive ourselves about money so easily. Purify us, we pray, from a love of money, so that you might be our undisputed King. Help us to love you with all our heart, soul, mind, and strength. And yes, with our money, as well. In Jesus' name, we pray. Amen.

10. Temptation to Worry (6:25-34)

Matthew 6:19-34 contains many contrasts:

- 6:19-20 - **Heavenly treasures vs. Earthly treasures**
- 6:22-23 - **Good eyes vs. Bad eyes**
- 6:23 – **Light vs. Darkness**
- 6:24 – **God vs. Money**
- 6:25-30 – **Worry vs. Faith**
- 6:31-33 - **Seeking earthly things vs. Seeking God's kingdom**

Harry Hanley Parker (1869-1917), detail of "Sermon on the Mount" (1905), mural, Calvary United Methodist Church, West Philadelphia. Center panel.

Let's examine some of these contrasts.

Money has the potential to derail our spiritual life disastrously. How we think about and handle our money is not just a personal matter, it is a discipleship matter. That is why Jesus spends time teaching about its twin evils – the temptation for money to become the:

1. Focus of our life, another master, another god (6:19-24), and
2. Focus of our worries and cares and thus consume our joy and life direction (6:25-34).

Jesus is speaking about materialism. The English dictionary defines materialism as "a theory that physical matter is the only or fundamental reality and that all being and processes and phenomena can be explained as manifestations or results of matter." Also "a preoccupation with or stress upon material rather than spiritual or intellectual things."[1]

Anatomy of Anxiety

This section's passage 6:25-34 examines how worry about money can erode our very faith. Notice in verse 30b, Jesus chides those who worry for their "little faith." Undue worry ought to be viewed as a lack of faith, something to be overcome.

First, let's look at the word "worry." The KJV uses the phrase "take no thought" a

[1] *Merriam Webster's 11th Collegiate Dictionary.*

number of times in this passage, but that translation can be misleading. NASB and RSV use "do not be anxious." NIV and NRSV render it "do not worry." The Greek word is *merimnaō*, "to be apprehensive, have anxiety, be anxious, be (unduly) concerned."[2] And it conforms well to the English definition of worry: "mental distress or agitation resulting from concern, usually for something impending or anticipated, anxiety."[3]

Illustrations of the Father's Care (6:26, 28-30, 32)

Jesus gives two illustrations of his Father's care for the disciples, and it centers upon value. First, he points them to the birds:

> "Look at the birds of the air; they do not sow or reap or store away in barns, and yet your heavenly Father feeds them. Are you not much more valuable than they?" (6:26)

The birds are under the Father's care. Not one falls to the ground without the Father knowing about it, yet a pair of sparrows could be purchased for a penny in the market (Matthew 10:29).

Then he points them to the flowers:

> "See how the lilies of the field grow. They do not labor or spin. Yet I tell you that not even Solomon in all his splendor was dressed like one of these." (6:28-29)

Q1. (Matthew 6:26-30) What point does Jesus make with his twin Parables of the Birds of the Air and of the Flowers of the Field? Is the point trivial or is it valid?
http://www.joyfulheart.com/forums/index.php?showtopic=774

May in Northern California is a glorious time. The blue lupine has reached its zenith and covers the fields in blue tinged with purple vetch. But it doesn't last for long. Soon the first winds of a hot summer begin to blow. So it was in the similar climate of Palestine. Very quickly, these gorgeous flowers lose their blossoms and are burned with the grasses for fuel. The point here is that since the Father provides for the *least* valuable, how much more will he care for the *very* valuable – us.

What Worry Can't Do (6:27)

We should have a wise concern for the future and take whatever steps we need to now to provide for ourselves and our families. Farmers have done that for thousands of

---

[2] *Merimnaō*, BDAG 632.
[3] *Merriam Webster's 11th Collegiate Dictionary*.

years – saving seed and planting crops for future harvest.

But what Jesus is addressing here is the kind of destructive anxiety that eats into our souls and deprives us of sleep. Anxiety that robs us of our present peace and joy, and propels us into a mythical future where we lack what we need, where we are gripped by fear – and which often is only that, a myth. Many of our fears and worries never materialize, and our worrying seldom has anything to do with fixing or repairing the future, only fearing it.

Jesus recognized the impotence of worry:

> "Who of you by worrying can add a single hour to his life?" (6:27)

This verse contains a word that can have two possible translations: Greek *hēlikia*: "the period of time that one's life continues, age, time of life." Or "bodily stature."[4] So KJV has, "... add one cubit unto his stature," while NIV and other modern translations are a bit more figurative: "... add a single hour to his life." No matter how you take it, the point is the same: our worrying accomplishes nothing at all.

Worry Is Sin (6:30-32)

This corrosive worry is thinly disguised unbelief. Jesus says:

> "[30] If that is how God clothes the grass of the field, which is here today and tomorrow is thrown into the fire, will he not much more clothe you, O you of **little faith**? [31] So do not worry, saying, 'What shall we eat?' or 'What shall we drink?' or 'What shall we wear?' [32] For the pagans run after all these things, and your heavenly Father knows that you need them." (6:30-32)

In verses 31-32, Jesus notes that the "pagans" or "Gentiles" (*ethnos*) also seek after food and clothing. Believers ought to be different somehow!

Worry is a sign of little faith. Faith and anxiety are opposites, and Christians are to open their lives to faith and to reject worry. Worry involves the constant fretting and anxiety that results from thinking about future problems. We Christians are to grow out of that habit. The Apostle Paul tells us how to do that:

> "Do not be anxious about anything, but in everything, by prayer and petition, with thanksgiving, present your requests to God. And the peace of God, which transcends all understanding, will guard your hearts and your minds in Christ Jesus. Finally, brothers, whatever is true, whatever is noble, whatever is right, whatever is pure, whatever is lovely, whatever is admirable – if anything is excellent or praiseworthy – think about these things." (Philippians 4:6-7)

---

[4] *Hēlikia*, BDAG 435-436, meanings 1a and possibly 3.

These two verses spell out the steps to escape worry's death grip. They require disciplining our minds and thoughts, something that even worldly people have realized is a prerequisite to success:

1. **Pray, bring your worries to God**. Instead of letting your worries rattle around in your mind, formulate them into prayers and petitions to your Father.

2. **Pray with thanksgiving**. Thanksgiving for what? For what God has done in the past. When we take time to praise God for who he is and what he has done in the past, we are encouraged and strengthened to believe he will do that for us in the future as well. Praise is the language of faith and stirs up faith.

3. **Turn your thoughts** away from topics of anxiety to those good and noble thoughts that will bring you peace.

Q2. (Matthew 6:25-34) How many times in this passage does the phrase "do not worry," "do not be anxious," or "take no thought" occur? In what way does excessive worry border on sin? Are worry and trust exact opposites?
http://www.joyfulheart.com/forums/index.php?showtopic=775

Q3. (Matthew 6:31-32) Why does Jesus mention the "pagans" or "Gentiles" in verse 32? What point is he making? How should a Christian differ from a Gentile, according to Jesus' teaching in this passage? What emotional and faith effect does the phrase, "your heavenly Father knows that you need them," have in *your* life?
http://www.joyfulheart.com/forums/index.php?showtopic=776

Seeking God (6:32-33)

"32 For the pagans **seek after** (*epizēteō*) all these things, and your heavenly Father knows that you need them.

33 But **seek** (*zēteō*) first his kingdom and his righteousness, and all these things will be given to you as well. 34 Therefore do not worry about tomorrow, for tomorrow will worry about itself. Each day has enough trouble of its own." (Matthew 6:32-33)

People are always seeking something. In verses 32-33 two words for "seek, seek after" occur.

The Greek verb *zēteō*, means "to seek, look for." Here it has the connotation: "to devote serious effort to realize one's desire or objective, strive for, aim (at), try to obtain, desire, wish (for), desire to possess (something)."[5] NRSV renders it, "But strive first for the kingdom of God...."

So what is it you seek? Pagans or Gentile unbelievers seek after temporal things – food, drink, clothing. What's more, Jesus says, "your heavenly Father knows that you need them." They aren't bad things. But they can preoccupy our "seeking" so we do not have time, energy, or interest to seek the Source of those things – God himself. Jesus taught:

> "The worries of this life and the deceitfulness of wealth choke [the Word], making it unfruitful." (Matthew 13:22)

Seek God First and Foremost (6:33)

> "But seek first his kingdom and his righteousness, and all these things will be given to you as well." (6:33)

The difference, then, between the disciple and others is that the disciple seeks God first. He or she gives priority to God first. This is the same issue that Jesus touched on in 6:21 – "Where your treasure is, there your heart will be also." We seek first what we treasure most. He also touched on it in 6:24 – "No one can serve two masters ... You cannot serve God and Money." We are not to seek our welfare and God with equal intensity. The great Quest for God must be first and foremost, not relegated to religion or Sunday practice, "... that in all things he might have the preeminence" (Colossians 1:18b).

Seeking God's Kingdom and Righteousness (6:33)

The object of our seeking is to be two-fold, according to Jesus.

First, we are to seek God's kingdom or God's reign in our lives and in his world. In the Lord's prayer we are taught to pray,

> "Your kingdom come, your will be done on earth as it is in heaven" (6:10).

We are not only to pray for it, but seek for it to come about.

Some are longing only to leave this earth and get to the peace of heaven. But the disciple is to seek for God's kingdom here on earth, too. Will it come? After World War I, "the war to end all wars," many Christians saw things as getting better and better, and a belief in the post-millennial reign of Christ was popular. Then World War II revealed the evil in man and in the world, and pessimism set in. Now Christians were longing for

---

[5] *Zēteō*, BDAG 428, 3.a.

the pre-millennial Rapture, just to get away.

While I agree that the Kingdom will not come completely until Christ rules literally on the earth (Revelation 20:4), I believe that we Christians are to seek God's Kingdom in the here and now and not be satisfied with the reign of evil. We are to be salt and light in the earth (Matthew 5:13-14). We are to be leaven in the loaf (Matthew 13:33). We are to be agents of change – faith-filled followers of the Miracle Worker from Galilee who left changed lives in his wake. We are to seek the Kingdom of God.[6]

Second, we are to seek God's righteousness. Much of Matthew 5 in the Sermon on the Mount compares the Pharisaic understanding of legalistic righteousness with Jesus' heart righteousness which is the spirit of the Law. We are to seek the impossible righteousness that resonates with Jesus' command: "Be perfect, therefore, as your heavenly Father is perfect" (5:48). This kind of heart righteousness is not the stuff of religious observance alone. Nor ritual. Nor even righteous deeds. It comes from a persistent, insistent, thirsty seeking after God. It comes from a dissatisfaction with our own imperfections until we let him break our hardness of heart and then mold us more fully into his image. A simple song expresses this heart Quest:

> "Spirit of the Living God, fall afresh on me.
> Spirit of the Living God, fall afresh on me.
> Melt me, mold me, fill me, use me!
> Spirit of the Living God, fall afresh on me."[7]

Ultimately it is not a self-produced righteousness that we seek. It is a righteousness that he works in us, that is, the personal righteousness that is the fruit of Christ's righteousness imputed to us by faith (Philippians 3:9).

For so long we have sought everything else – food, shelter, advancement. Seek Him first, says the Discipler.

> "Seek first God's Kingdom and his righteousness, and all these things shall be added unto you." (6:33)

---

[6] Some more recent translations such as the NIV, RSV, and NASB do not include the words "of God," since these words are missing in a number of early and important manuscripts (Aleph, B, etc.). However, in an interesting change of scholarly opinion, the editorial committee of the United Bible Societies' Greek New Testament explains the absence of "of God" as an accidental scribal omission, and includes "of God" in their text, though in brackets to reflect some uncertainty. This is now reflected in the NRSV which restores the full phrase "kingdom of God." (Bruce M. Metzger, A Textual Commentary on the Greek New Testament (United Bible Societies, 1971), pp. 18-19.)

[7] "Spirit of the Living God," words and music by Dan Iverson (©1935. Renewed 1963 Birdwing Music)

All these things will be given to you as well (6:33b)

So many people seek happiness with their whole being yet somehow never seem to attain it. It is ephemeral. But when we seek God, wherever and however he leads us, we can see and taste his Kingdom and his righteousness *and* we find that he meets our temporal needs, too.

Sometimes I think of Jesus' tragic words:

> "What good will it be for a man if he gains the whole world, yet forfeits his soul? Or what can a man give in exchange for his soul?" (Matthew 16:26)

Searching for the wrong thing first will damn us. We disciples must set our eyes towards one great Quest, and one only: "Seek first the Kingdom of God and his righteousness," and with it comes a promise: "and all these things will be given to you as well."

The word translated "be added" or "be given" is the future passive of Greek *prostithēmi*, "'add, put to," here with the connotation, "to add as a benefit, provide, give, grant, do."[8] He will add to our Kingdom-seeking the other things that we need. He will quench our spiritual thirst *and* our natural one as well.

Ultimately this Quest is a faith-Quest that sorts out priorities and settles upon the one great goal of seeking God first. God takes care of the rest and will not disappoint us, if our heart is rightly placed. Just as he feeds the birds and clothes the flowers, he will meet all our needs, too.

Labor Still Needed

Can we take this passage as an excuse not to work for a living? Of course not. Jesus was well aware, I am sure, that birds still had to find and gather their food. In our scientific age we know that flowers must still grow by manufacturing tissue using the elements in the air and the ground by means of photosynthesis. Work is not excluded. The point is that God provides for their needs.

Watchcare Still Needed

Though God supplies food and clothing, shelter and "everything we need for life and godliness" (2 Peter 1:3), that is no reason for us to focus exclusively on ourselves and not be concerned about the needs of others. Scientists who have studied famines have come to an interesting conclusion: the problem is not that there is not enough food, but that there is a distribution problem. Distributing food to starving villages in the Sudan or to

---

[8] *Prostithēmi*, BDAG 885, 2.

refugees in Bangladesh requires compassion and, often, a will to resist the evil of corrupt rulers who would deprive their citizens of basic needs to accomplish their own selfish political purposes.

Jesus acknowledged that we will always have the poor with us (Matthew 26:11), but affirms that we are obligated to help them as we are able:

> "For I was hungry and you gave me something to eat, I was thirsty and you gave me something to drink, I was a stranger and you invited me in, I needed clothes and you clothed me, I was sick and you looked after me, I was in prison and you came to visit me.... I tell you the truth, whatever you did for one of the least of these brothers of mine, you did for me." (Matthew 25:35-36, 40)

Indeed, sometimes we are the essential means that the Father uses to provide clothing and food to his children. "Your heavenly Father knows that we need them" (6:32) and he uses his servants to help supply the needs of his other children.

Q4. (Matthew 6:33) What is the command in this verse? How must our seeking God differ from our seeking of food and clothing, according to this verse? What is the promise found in this verse?
http://www.joyfulheart.com/forums/index.php?showtopic=777

Tomorrow Will Worry about Itself (6:34)

> "Therefore do not worry about tomorrow, for tomorrow will worry about itself. Each day has enough trouble of its own." (6:34)

Worry, worry, worry. We fall so easily into churning about the future. Worry, you see, is always future. You don't worry about the now, you just live in it. You can only worry about the future. However, we can deal with worry by turning our eyes toward the One Quest for God's Kingdom and righteousness. That is the focus of our future.

Jesus concludes this part of the Sermon on the Mount with a touch of humor: "Tomorrow will worry about itself." Oh, I know some sober-sides contend that Jesus never smiled, but we know better. I find it hard to believe that Jesus uttered this phrase without more than a hint of a smile. Perhaps a chuckle, too. Think about the silliness of tomorrow worrying all by itself and maybe you'll get the joke.

His final observation is: "Each day has enough trouble of its own." What he is saying is that we don't need to go borrowing trouble from tomorrow; we have enough already. Deal with today by God's help. Then tomorrow, deal with tomorrow, and he'll help you there, too. Alcoholics Anonymous rightly has adopted as a slogan, "Take one day at a time." Yes, that sums up Jesus' teaching here very well.

Q5. (Matthew 6:34) Is there humor intended in verse 34? What is the point of Jesus' joke here? What is the command in this verse?
http://www.joyfulheart.com/forums/index.php?showtopic=778

Every Easter Sunday many churches sing that Bill and Gloria Gaither song, "Because He Lives." It expresses so well the comradeship we have with God that replaces our worry with something divine:

"Because He lives I can face tomorrow;
Because He lives all fear is gone;
Because I know He holds the future,
And life is worth the living just because He lives."[9]

Prayer

Lord, sometimes I get so distracted by everyday life that I forget to talk to you about it. Forgive me. Help me to seek you constantly – your presence, your help, your wisdom, your mercy. Let my life revolve around you, your righteousness, and your Kingdom. In Jesus' name, I pray. Amen.

---

[9] "Because He Lives," words and music by William and Gloria Gaither (© 1971 by William J. Gaither, ARR UBP of Gaither Copyright Management)

V. Discernment in the Kingdom (7:1-29)

The final chapter of the Sermon on the Mount is much harder to organize by themes than chapters 5 and 6. I've called 7:1-29 "Discernment in the Kingdom." Verses 1-6 discuss discerning self and others. Verses 7-12 explain discernment with regard to faith. Verses 7:13-29 comment on discerning the true way. I think that's a stretch. But though the teachings in Chapter 7 are hard to group, they are vital to our understanding as disciples. Some are difficult to understand at first. We'll consider them in three chapters:

11. Judging Self and Others (7:1-6)

12. Asking in Faith (7:7-12)

13. Enter the Narrow Gate (7:13-28)

Dante Gabriel Rossetti, "The Sermon on the Mount" (1862), Stained glass window, south nave, All Saints, Selsley, Gloucestershire, UK.

11. Judging Self and Others (7:1-6)

Judge Not (7:1)

Probably one of the most misquoted and misused verses in the New Testament is found in verse 1 of our passage:

> "Do not judge, or you too will be judged." (7:1)

It is a hard saying. Can it mean what it seems to? So often I hear people chiding any negative statement with this verse. If we can't make critical judgments, doesn't our ability to choose between good and evil disappear?

Perhaps the best New Testament image self-righteous judgmentalism is the Pharisees pressing Jesus to condemn a sinful women. Lucas Cranach the Younger, "Christ and the Woman Taken in Adultery" (after 1532), oil on copperplate, The Hermitage, St. Petersburg.

The basic meaning of the Greek word for judge (*krinō*) is "to set apart so as to distinguish, separate." Then, by transference, "select" and "pass judgment upon."[1] The word is used in the New Testament to refer to all kinds of judging, and such a broad definition doesn't refine our understanding much.

Next, we go to the context, and find that it seems to limit the usage of the word. Jesus requires of his disciples several critical judgments in this chapter:

1. "First take the plank out of your own eye, and then you will see clearly to remove the speck from your brother's eye" (7:5). Both discerning the plank in your own eye and then discerning the speck in your brother's require critical judgment.

2. "Do not give dogs what is sacred; do not throw your pearls to pigs" (7:6a). Jesus expects us to discern "dogs" and "pigs."

---

[1] *Krinō*, BDAG 567-569.

3. "Watch out for false prophets. They come to you in sheep's clothing, but inwardly they are ferocious wolves. By their fruit you will recognize them" (7:15-16). Jesus expects his followers to discern false prophets from true ones.

So the command "Do not judge" cannot prohibit all critical judgments.

Notice, too, that the context here is "brothers" (7:3, 5), fellow believers. Jesus is speaking about the kind of judgmental attitude that can spring up among religious people within the religious community. You've seen it: picky, picky, picky. No one is quite good enough to please them. Some men and women act as if they have the spiritual gift of criticism.

If you look even more carefully, you see that we are not prohibited from discerning sin or problems in our brother, or even seeking to correct them. But we must first examine ourselves to make sure nothing in us prevents us from seeing clearly. Then, and then only, says Jesus, you can "see clearly to remove the speck from your brother's eye" (7:5).

Projection and Censoriousness

Psychologists describe the phenomenon of "projection," defined as "the attribution of one's own ideas, feelings, or attitudes to other people or to objects; especially, the externalization of blame, guilt, or responsibility as a defense against anxiety."[2] Jesus' comments on judgmentalism are given right after a discourse on worry or anxiety. Interesting.

We saw a sad example of this a number of years ago when televangelist Jim Baker's sexual sins were exposed. Who was one of the loudest critics? Televangelist Jimmy Swaggart, whose own sexual sins were exposed a few months later. I've seen this kind of behavior occur throughout my own ministry. Those who are most critical tend to be those who condemn themselves for the very same sins. In condemning others, they are affirming their self-condemnation and self-loathing.

Jesus does not require us to suspend our critical faculties. But he is warning us not to be censorious or quick to criticize, since our judgmental attitude may reflect our own sins more than our brothers' sins.

So how should we understand verse 1? J.B. Phillips renders it, "Don't criticize people, and you will not be criticized."[3] In *The Message*, Eugene H. Peterson paraphrases it, "Don't pick on people, jump on their failures, criticize their faults – unless, of course,

---

[2] *Merriam Webster's 11th Collegiate Dictionary.*
[3] J.B. Phillips, *The New Testament in Modern English* (Macmillan, 1958).

you want the same treatment."[4]

John Stott prefers the English word "censoriousness,"[5] marked by or given to cen-
sure.[6] This is exactly it – not an objective, discerning judgment, but the harshness of one
who is a fault-finder, a blamer, one who puts the worst possible construction upon an
act, one who condemns sternly.

**Q1. (Matthew 7:1) Have you ever caught yourself severely criticizing others Christians
behind their backs – or to their faces? What is the attitude that underlies censoriousness? How can the psychological concept of "projection" motivate harsh judgment?
Why must Christians show love in the face of a brother's or sister's failing?**
http://www.joyfulheart.com/forums/index.php?showtopic=779

Healing and Restoration

Wouldn't it be refreshing to be part of a church where brothers and sisters would
encourage one another to love and good works, and be very gentle with one another's
weaknesses? Yes, our obligation as brothers and sisters is to help one another escape
from sin, but we need to carry out this duty very carefully and lovingly, like fine eye
surgery:

> "Brothers, if someone is caught in a sin, **you who are spiritual should restore him
> gently**. But watch yourself, or you also may be tempted. Carry each other's burdens,
> and in this way you will fulfill the law of Christ." (Galatians 6:1-2)

The Measure You Use (7:1b-2)

Now let's look at the second half of verse 1, "... or you too will be judged." Judged by
whom? J.B. Phillips assigns it to others, a kind of "what goes around, comes around"
philosophy. But I don't agree. I think Jesus is talking about God's judgment of us. It goes
back to the principle of 6:14-15 that if we withhold forgiveness of others, then the Father
won't forgive our sins. David Hill comments, "The meaning is that, if you condemn, you
exclude yourself from God's pardon."[7] Other commentators agree.

"With the measure you use, it will be measured to you [by God]" (7:2).

---

[4] Eugene G. Peterson, *The Message: The New Testament in Contemporary Language* (NavPress, 1993).
[5] Stott, *Message*, p. 176.
[6] *Merriam Webster's 11th Collegiate Dictionary*.
[7] David Hill, *Gospel of Matthew* (New Century Bible Commentary, Eerdmans, 1972), p. 146.

We see a similar use of the idea of measuring in Luke's gospel:

> "Give, and it will be given to you. A good measure, pressed down, shaken together and running over, will be poured into your lap. For with the measure you use, it will be measured to you." (Luke 6:38)

Here Jesus talks about kinds of measures. I think of sets of measuring cups and measuring spoons in our modern-day kitchens. There are various sizes. In this passage there is no doubt that God is the one who will measure out the blessing to you in accordance with the measure with which you give.

Q2. (Matthew 7:1-2) Read a similar passage in Luke 6:37-38. According to Matthew's account, what is our fate if we measure out big heaps of judgment with a critical spirit? According to Luke's account, how can measuring be both positive and negative? What should we measure out instead of judgmentalism?
http://www.joyfulheart.com/forums/index.php?showtopic=780

Judgment Day for Christians

If we measure out criticism to our brothers, then God will measure out criticism to us on Judgment Day. If we measure out blessing and encouragement, then that will be measured out to us. If we use a tiny measuring cup, we will receive a tiny recompense. But if we heap on the criticism, then we can expect a heaped up judgment on ourselves.

This makes some evangelical Christians uncomfortable. To them it smacks of "works righteousness." We would like to escape any judgment, even though the scripture is quite clear that even Christians will be judged for what we do in the body (Romans 14:10; 1 Corinthians 4:3-5; 2 Corinthians 5:10). We will be rewarded for that which is worthy, and our rewards will be stripped from us for that which is unworthy. Paul writes, for example,

> "... His work will be shown for what it is, because the Day will bring it to light. It will be revealed with fire, and the fire will test the quality of each man's work. If what he has built survives, he will receive his reward. If it is burned up, he will suffer loss; he himself will be saved, but only as one escaping through the flames." (1 Corinthians 3:13-15)

Now you can see why the epithet, "God damn you," is so damning. When we call down God's judgment on others, we risk calling down the same kind of judgment for our own sins, for "with the measure you use, it will be measured to you." It certainly behooves us to examine ourselves carefully before proceeding.

Why is it that Christians are sometimes the most harsh and strident and self-righteous people? Because they don't take seriously Jesus' clear teaching in this passage.

Sawdust Specks and Timber Beams (7:3-5)

I find it hard to believe that Jesus said verses 3-5 with a straight face. The comparison is intended to be funny. Picture a man with a large plank of timber in his eye stooping down to perform minute eye surgery on a man with only a sawdust speck in his eye.

Yet that is what we do when we try to correct others without careful self-examination and surrender so that God can cleanse our own lives. Jesus calls those who are quick to correct others without correcting themselves "hypocrites," and enjoins them to take the plank out of their own eye first.

Jesus' classic parable on this contrast is the Parable of the Pharisee and the Tax Collector.

> "To some who were confident of their own righteousness and looked down on every-body else, Jesus told this parable: Two men went up to the temple to pray, one a Phari-see and the other a tax collector. The Pharisee stood up and prayed about himself: 'God, I thank you that I am not like other men–robbers, evildoers, adulterers–or even like this tax collector. I fast twice a week and give a tenth of all I get.'

> "But the tax collector stood at a distance. He would not even look up to heaven, but beat his breast and said, 'God, have mercy on me, a sinner.'

> "I tell you that this man, rather than the other, went home justified before God. For everyone who exalts himself will be humbled, and he who humbles himself will be exalted." (Luke 18:9-14)

Before criticizing someone else we need to humble ourselves before God and repent of our own sins. Then in humility, we can serve others in genuine love, rather than genuine pride. Notice, in Matthew 7:5, *after* they remove the plank from their own eye, then they can see clearly to help their brother. They probably also have a good idea of how painful this surgery is and will be extremely gentle and understanding.

Q3. (Matthew 7:3-5) What about this parable is humorous? Why do you think Jesus compares a speck of sawdust with a plank or beam? What does the speck represent? What does the plank represent? According to this parable, when is it okay to remove a speck? When is it not okay?

http://www.joyfulheart.com/forums/index.php?showtopic=781

Pigs and Dogs (7:6)

Verse 6 is also difficult to grasp:

> "Do not give dogs what is sacred; do not throw your pearls to pigs. If you do, they may
> trample them under their feet, and then turn and tear you to pieces" (7:6).

One of the keys is to understand the view of dogs and pigs in Hebrew culture. Pigs, of course, were considered unclean animals; Jews were forbidden to eat pork of any kind. Only Gentiles raised pigs (Matthew 8:30-34).

We think of a dog as "man's best friend," but that was by no means the view of the period we are studying. Rather they were scavengers around the towns and cities. They might eat the decaying flesh of carcasses in the wild, which would have deeply offended the Jews' understanding of holiness and ritual cleanness. Dogs are looked down on in verses like Proverbs 26:11 and Matthew 15:26-27. The Jews also used the word "dogs" to refer to Gentile outsiders (compare Philippians 3:2 and Revelation 22:15).

Can you imagine giving holy food from the temple to an unclean dog scavenger? Of course not! Pearls were extremely precious. To throw them into the pig pen would be to not only lose them in the slime, but also to anger the pig, who might come after you for throwing him inedible food.

So who are the dogs and swine Jesus is referring to? They seem to be people who openly reject the gospel of Christ. Consider these verses:

> "If anyone will not welcome you or listen to your words, shake the dust off your feet
> when you leave that home or town." (Matthew 10:14)

> "When the Jews saw the crowds, they were filled with jealousy and talked abusively
> against what Paul was saying.... The Jews incited the God-fearing women of high stand-
> ing and the leading men of the city. They stirred up persecution against Paul and Barna-
> bas, and expelled them from their region. So they shook the dust from their feet in
> protest against them and went to Iconium." (Acts 13:44-45, 50-51)

> "When the Jews opposed Paul and became abusive, [Paul] shook out his clothes in
> protest and said to them, 'Your blood be on your own heads! I am clear of my responsi-
> bility. From now on I will go to the Gentiles.'" (Acts 18:5-6)

Jesus is instructing his disciples to discern those who reject the gospel outright, and not to continue to declare it to them so that it is continually slandered and discredited. Rather, go to those who are receptive and hungry for hope.

Q4. (Matthew 7:6) In Jesus' day, what did dogs and pigs have in common? What would holy food and pearls have in common? Read Matthew 10:14; Acts 13:44-51; 18:5-6; and 28:17-28. In what kinds of circumstances did believers turn away from a continued sharing of the gospel? To what kinds of people did they continue their witness?

http://www.joyfulheart.com/forums/index.php?showtopic=782

In summary, Jesus teaches us to be slow to judge our fellow believers, and to be careful to examine our own hearts before presuming to correct them. On the other hand, he calls on disciples to discern the hearts of unbelievers, and refuse to continually preach to those who reject, who show themselves to be like unclean animals, unworthy of the Good News.

It is Good News though, make no mistake. And its goodness includes forgiving and cleansing even those whom we condemn and criticize. If we let it, the Good News of God's mercy can extend to our own hearts, as well, displacing the caustic tongue with love and graciousness. God grant it!

Prayer

Lord, I can't count the times when I've had to stop myself from harsh criticism of a brother or a sister. I'm guilty of this kind of judgmentalism. Forgive me. Make my lips sweet with love and grace. And show your grace to me in my sin. In Jesus' name, I pray. Amen.

12. Asking in Faith (7:7-12)

Earlier in the Sermon on the Mount, Jesus warned his disciples against formal, hypocritical prayer, and gave them a model prayer to start them on their prayer journey. Now he takes the lesson a step further by teaching them to ask in faith. The teaching seems to be simple – and at one level it is. Meditate with me on these words.

Jesus introduces three words that indicate desire that would be met: ask, seek, and knock.

Ask (7:7-8)

Ask seems to refer to simple petition, with the promise "it will be given to

Carl Heinrich Bloch (Danish painter, 1834-1890), "Consolator," oil on canvas, public collection.

you." The verb is *aiteō*, "to ask for, with a claim on receipt of an answer, ask, ask for, demand."[1] Many of our prayers are of this kind. Finding that parents are the key to getting many things, our children commonly ask for what they want: "Mom, can I have some cookies." Or "Dad, can I drive the car tonight?"

The answer, though, is not so simple. It could be, "Yes, I'll bring some to you on a plate." Or, "No, they'll spoil your dinner." Or, "Not now, but after you finish your math homework you can take a break and have three cookies – no more."

Jesus illustrates this type of prayer in verses 9-11: "Which of you, if his son asks for bread, will give him a stone?" The son asks for bread, and he is given bread.

---

[1] *Aiteō*, BDAG 30.

But the answer is not always what we want to hear. No child wants to hear "No" or "Not now," even though those may be the only "good gift" options, and answering the child with the exact thing that he asked may prove to be not a "good gift" at all. Children have such narrow perspectives and frames of reference – don't we!

But Jesus tells us to ask, expecting an answer. James amplifies this for us:

> "You want something but don't get it.... You do not have, because you do not ask God. When you ask, you do not receive, because you ask with wrong motives, that you may spend what you get on your pleasures." (James 4:2-3)

One of the lessons Jesus is teaching us is to ask for the things we desire, rather than just trying to seize them on our own. One thing we eventually learn as children is that for some things the answer is always, "No." We learn not to ask any further. We also learn that in some areas if we ask, and conditions are right, we will receive. As we listen to our parents, we are educated in what to ask for and how to ask.

We don't learn these things by never asking. We learn by continuing to ask, and gradually learning our parents' mind, and asking according to what we perceive to be their mind. The Apostle John wrote,

> "This is the confidence we have in approaching God: that if we ask anything according to his will, he hears us. And if we know that he hears us – whatever we ask – we know that we have what we asked of him." (1 John 5:14-15)

We are told to ask.

Alexandre Bida (French painter, 1823-1895), detail from "A Woman Healed by Touching the Garment of Jesus," engraving, in Edward Eggleston, *Christ in Art* (New York: Fords, Howard, & Hulbert, 1874).

Seek (7:7-8)

"Ask" indicates a petition. "Seek," however, indicates a search for something that is either lost or has not yet been found or discovered. The verb is *zēteō*, "try to find something, seek, look for," with the possible additional sense of "devote serious effort to realize one's desire or objective, strive for, aim (at), try to obtain, desire, wish (for)."[2]

---

[2] *Zēteō*, BDAG 428, 1a., perhaps 3a.

"Seek, and you will find," Jesus says.

Just previously in the Sermon on the Mount, he had instructed his disciples, "Seek first the kingdom of God and his righteousness, and all these things will be given to you as well" (6:33). It is as if Jesus calls his disciples to a Quest for a kingdom and righteousness that are not immediately obvious.

One of the traditions at our house after church on Easter morning is for all the children – and the Daddy – to search for Easter baskets filled with candy that the Mommy has hidden. My children have bright eyes, I guess. Because they inevitably find theirs before I find mine. The children will spot mine. "Dad, why can't you see it. It's right in front of you." I look high and low, but it usually takes a clue, or the "You're-Getting-Warmer" Game for me to find it.

Seeking can be frustrating, but we must not give up. Jesus has told us to seek his kingdom and his righteousness. I also recall verses from the Prophets where God says,

> "The lions may grow weak and hungry,
> but those who **seek the Lord** lack no good thing." (Psalm 34:10)

> "You will seek me and find me
> when you **seek me with all your heart**." (Jeremiah 29:13)

> "Then I will go back to my place
> until they admit their guilt.
> And they will **seek my face**;
> in their misery they will earnestly seek me." (Hosea 5:15)

> "**Seek me and live**;
> do not seek Bethel,
> do not go to Gilgal,
> do not journey to Beersheba....
> Seek the Lord and live...." (Amos 5:4-6)

> "**Seek the Lord while he may be found**;
> call on him while he is near.
> Let the wicked forsake his way
> and the evil man his thoughts.
> Let him turn to the Lord, and he will have mercy on him,
> and to our God, for he will freely pardon.
> For my thoughts are not your thoughts,
> neither are your ways my ways,"
> declares the Lord.
> As the heavens are higher than the earth,
> so are my ways higher than your ways

and my thoughts than your thoughts." (Isaiah 55:6-9)

The seeking process is a maturing process, a sifting process, and – if we continue and don't give up – becomes a single-minded Quest to know God. "Seek, and you will find." There is a promise here that if we will seek to know the Lord, and seek after his presence and blessing, we will find it. There is a looking that can be frustrating, but we are not to give up because we will find Him if we seek him with all our heart.

Knock (7:7-8)

The third command is "Knock,[3] and the door will be opened to you." Basically, knocking is confined to closed doors, not open ones. You've faced closed doors in your life, ones you sought desperately to open or reopen. Some of them you have banged on again and again. But then you learn to try other doors to see which one God will open.

In the New Testament, an "open door" seems to denote an "opportunity":

> "On arriving there, they gathered the church together and reported all that God had done through them and how he had **opened the door of faith** to the Gentiles." (Acts 14:27)

> "But I will stay on at Ephesus until Pentecost, because **a great door** for effective work **has opened to me**, and there are many who oppose me." (1 Corinthians 16:8-9)

> "Now when I went to Troas to preach the gospel of Christ and found that the Lord had **opened a door for me**...." (2 Corinthians 2:12)

> "And pray for us, too, that God may **open a door for our message**, so that we may proclaim the mystery of Christ, for which I am in chains." (Colossians 4:3)

"Knock," says Jesus, "and the door will be opened to you." We are to continue to knock on doors until God opens to us the opportunity he has in mind.

Continuous Action (7:7)

Jesus' teaching in verse 7 is in the form of a command. Grammatically, this is known as the Imperative Mood. In Greek, commands can be given in two tenses: Aorist tense commands indicate an immediate and single action ("Shut the door!"). Present tense commands, on the other hand, carry the idea of continuous and habitual action ("Always shut the door!" or "Keep on shutting the door!"). Each of the commands in verse 7 are in present tense imperative, and therefore stress continued, persistent action. William Barclay translates verse 7:

---

[3] *Krouō*, "to deliver a blow against something, strike, knock," in our literature only of knocking at a door. (BDAG 570).

"Keep on asking, and it will be given you;
Keep on seeking, and you will find;
Keep on knocking, and it will be opened to you."[4]

Q1. (Matthew 7:7-8) What do the words "ask," "seek," and "knock" have in common? What distinguishes them from each other? Does one word convey more intensity than another? What is the significance of the present, continuous, imperative tense of these verbs?
http://www.joyfulheart.com/forums/index.php?showtopic=783

Parables of Persistence (Luke 11:5-10 and 18:1-6)

It's pretty clear that this emphasis on continuous action in prayer is part of what Jesus intended, since in Luke's Gospel a parable of persistence immediately precedes his saying "Ask and it will be given to you."

In Luke 11:5-10 Jesus tells a humorous story of a man who is bedded down with his wife and children. They've finally settled down, stopped crying and talking, and are all asleep. His neighbor has a guest arrive at midnight and doesn't have anything to feed him. Hosts in the Middle East are required to serve guests when they arrive. It is a necessity. But this neighbor host was out of bread. So he went next door and began knocking on the door. The man inside tells him to go away. But because he continues to knock and won't give up, and the racket threatens to wake up his children, the man gets up, finds a loaf of bread, and gives him what he wants.

The neighbor's boldness (KJV "importunity") is highlighted. This word in Greek is *anaideia*, "a lack of sensitivity to what is proper, careless about the good opinion of others, shamelessness, impertinence, impudence, ignoring of convention."[5]

Jesus tells a similar parable in Luke 18:1-6. A widow has been cheated out of her rights by a crooked judge, but she wouldn't quit. She keeps coming to him with her plea day after day, week after week. The judge is finally exhausted by it.

> "... Because this widow keeps bothering me (literally, "causes me trouble"), I will see that she gets justice, so that she won't eventually wear me out with her coming!'" (Luke 18:5)

---

[4] William Barclay, *Gospel of Matthew* (Daily Study Bible series; Edinburgh: St. Andrew Press, 1958), vol. 1, p. 273.
[5] *Anaideia*, BDAG 63.

The point of this parable, Luke tells us plainly, is "to show them that they should always pray and not give up" (Luke 18:1).

Jesus tells two parables, both with some humor. We are not to learn that God will only act if we harass him, or that he is unjust and will only give us what we ask if we pester him. The point is that we are to continue to pray and not give up.

There have been many times in Israel's history when conditions were bad. Where people were discouraged. Where they were ready to quit. But a prophet would come along who encouraged them to continue to seek God, and eventually the answer would come. In our lives, too, there are conditions that we want changed. Our instruction as Christians is to continue to pray, and not to give up. Ask! Seek! Knock!

Q2. (Matthew 7:7-8) Which lesson is taught in *both* the Parables of the Friend at Midnight (Luke 11:5-10) and the Widow and the Unjust Judge (Luke 18:1-6)? How do these relate to the commands in Matthew 7:7-8?
http://www.joyfulheart.com/forums/index.php?showtopic=784

Persistence and Faith

On occasion, I have heard a teaching, a very spiritual teaching I am sure, that goes like this: "If you really have faith, all you have to do is ask once and then trust God. To ask again is a sign of unbelief, that God didn't hear you the first time." While this sounds very pious, it is diametrically opposed to Jesus' clear teaching. We are to ask, and to go on asking, until we receive. This is not a sign of unbelief, Jesus tells us, but of faith. Indeed, if we don't continue to ask, Jesus asks, "When the Son of Man comes will he find faith on the earth?" (Luke 18:8). Faith consists of asking until we get the answer, since we believe strongly that God will give us what we seek.

Faith in God's Goodness (7:9-11)

Coming back to our passage in the Sermon on the Mount, next Jesus tells another silly parable:

> [9] "Which of you, if his son asks for bread, will give him a stone? [10] Or if he asks for a fish, will give him a snake? [11] If you, then, though you are evil, know how to give good gifts to your children, how much more will your Father in heaven give good gifts to those who ask him!" (7:9-11)

What do a bread and a stone have in common? They are both approximately the same shape. And a fish and a snake? They both have scales. Jesus is saying that we can trust God to give us good gifts, and not instead slip us something useless, or even dangerous. Like a good Father, we can trust him. Even normal parents – "evil" in comparison to God – give good gifts to their children, he argues. How much more God himself.

Why does Jesus say this?

Sometimes we are afraid to pray. We are afraid to pray for God's will for our lives in fear that God might send us to darkest Africa where there are bugs and mosquitoes. So we don't pray. We are afraid to pray for patience, because we've heard that when you ask for patience God will send all sorts of hardships upon you. And so on.

Sometimes we're afraid to pray because we really don't know how to pray. We don't know exactly what to pray for. What if I ask for the wrong thing, and God, literalist that he is, gives it to me? I am afraid.

Don't be afraid, Jesus says. Your fear is an impediment to your faith. Just ask your Father for what you want and trust him to answer wisely with what is good for you. Trust him. Trust him and ask in faith in his goodness.

Q3. (Matthew 7:9-11). What do these verses teach us about God's relationship to us? What do they teach about God's characteristic response toward us? How does this differ from a cynical view of God? Why is a positive understanding of God important to be able to pray with faith?
http://www.joyfulheart.com/forums/index.php?showtopic=785

The Golden Rule (7:12)

The passage concludes with the Golden Rule:

> "So in everything, do to others what you would have them do to you, for this sums up the Law and the Prophets." (7:12)

In other words, in light of God's goodness and faithfulness in giving good gifts to his children, so you too are to do good to others.

It has been called the Golden Rule, I suppose, since it is such a perfect guideline to show us how to act: We should treat others in the way we would like to be treated. Not in our sick self-destructiveness or dark moods that rationalize evil towards ourselves. But in the clear light of day, as children of a good and generous God, we are to treat others as we would like to be treated, "for this sums up the Law and the Prophets,"

Jesus concludes.

People have argued that the Golden Rule isn't unique to Jesus. Confucius said, "Do not to others what you would not wish done to yourself." The Stoics had a very similar saying. In the Old Testament Apocrypha we read, "Do not do to anyone what you yourself would hate."[6] Rabbi Hillel in 20 BC said, "What is hateful to you, do not do to anyone else. This is the whole law; all the rest is only commentary."[7]

But notice that each of these is in the negative, somehow limiting or prohibiting certain actions. Jesus' statement is in the positive, guiding and directing all our actions toward others. It is like the command, "Love your neighbor as yourself." It is not a negative limitation but a positive guideline, a high standard indeed.

Q4. (Matthew 7:12) In what way does the "Golden Rule" capsulize the message of the law and the prophets? This seems like a different "summary" of the law and the prophets than Jesus indicated in Matthew 22:37-39. How are they the same? How are they different?
http://www.joyfulheart.com/forums/index.php?showtopic=786

In this section of the Sermon on the Mount Jesus teaches his disciples about trusting in God's goodness by continuing to ask, and then by living out that goodness towards those around us. What an uplifting, freeing teaching! And when Pentecost Sunday rolls around, it is good to recall that especially good gift the Father has given to us – his Holy Spirit to dwell within us and empower us with the very life of God. Thank you.

Prayer

Father, help us to learn persistence in prayer, seriousness about our requests before you – and so obey Jesus in our prayers and our faith. Forgive us for wimpy, wispy prayers that we forget soon after praying them. Teach us to ask, to seek, to knock – continually. In Jesus' name, we pray. Amen

---

[6] *Tobit* 4:15 (NEB).
[7] Talmud, *Shabbath* 31a.

13. Enter the Narrow Gate (7:13-29)

Too often we Christians live in the land of gray, a land devoid of moral absolutes, a land that has so dulled the cutting edge of our faith that we have accepted lethargy and disobedience as our daily fare, and almost believe our own rationalizations. At the conclusion of Jesus' Sermon on the Mount, the Jesus Manifesto, we find a wake-up call, a call to listen and obey, a call to follow.

Jesus, the consummate teacher, conveys the urgency of his call in a series of word pairs that draw the issues sharply:

Carl Heinrich Bloch (Danish painter, 1834-1890), detail from "Sermon on the Mount"

Narrow gate – Wide gate (13)

Narrow path – Broad way (14)

Life – Destruction (13-14)

Few – Many (13-14)

Sheep – Wolves (15)

(True prophets) – False prophets (15)

Good fruit – Bad fruit (16-20)

Good tree – Bad tree (16-20)

Grapes – Thornbushes (16)

Figs – Thistles (16)

Doers of his will – Mere professors (21-23)

Wise man – Foolish man (24-27)

Rock – Sand (24-27)

Did not fall – Fell with a great crash (24-27)

This passage examines deceit and discernment, first at the level of the masses ("broad is the way"), then at the level of the congregation ("false prophets" who are "wolves in sheep's clothing"), and finally at the personal level where we can deceive ourselves into thinking that we can hear without obeying.

The Small Gate and the Narrow Way (7:13-14)

> "¹³ Enter through the narrow gate. For wide is the gate and broad is the road that leads to destruction, and many enter through it. ¹⁴ But small is the gate and narrow the road that leads to life, and only a few find it." (7:13-14)

Sometimes Christian salvation is portrayed in such generous terms that all people will be saved – even the devil. This kind of teaching is called "universalism." In the New Age Movement and some of its Eastern Religion roots we hear the view that there are many roads to God, and that the World's Great Teachers – Buddha, Moses, Jesus, Mohammed – all brought great truths, many of which are similar. There are many roads that lead to God, this teaching suggests. And eventually everyone finds God. Except, perhaps, for the evil few such as Hitler and the like.

But what Jesus teaches is much different – radically different. In verses 13-14 we see:

1. **A Command**: Enter through the narrow gate.

2. **An Explanation**:
   (a) For the gate is wide and the way broad that leads to destruction
   (b) And many enter through it.
   (c) But the gate is small and the path narrow that leads to life
   (d) And only a few find it.

The last sentence has two key phrases:

"Only a few..." We are impressed with numbers. Largest, greatest, most. Jesus isn't. We feel that majority opinion rules. Jesus walked his own lonely path. He called Twelve and named them apostles, and from those Twelve the Christian movement was born. At times in history the Christian movement has appeared to hang by a thread. One person, one small band of people. St. Patrick in Ireland or Adoniram Judson in Burma. If we are to learn to follow Jesus, we must be committed to following him where others will not go. Where we are scorned, alone, solitary.

"... find it." The second phrase is "find it." Finding something presupposes searching earnestly for it. Jesus has just taught, "Seek and you shall find." The way is clear only to those who search for it, for at times it doesn't not seem well-trodden, though many saints have walked that way.

Leads to Destruction (7:13)

The destination also is startling. One path leads to destruction, the other to life. What does "destruction" mean? The Greek word is *apōleia* means, "the 'destruction' that one experiences, 'annihilation' both complete and in process, 'ruin.'"[1] Whenever we see the word in the New Testament it seems to promise a terrible end:

"May your money **perish** with you..." (Acts 8:20)

"... Objects of his wrath, prepared for **destruction**." (Romans 9:22)

"This is a sign to them that they will be **destroyed**, but that you will be saved." (Philippians 1:28)

"Their destiny is **destruction**...." (Philippians 3:19)

"... The man of lawlessness is revealed, the man doomed to **destruction**." (2 Thessalonians 2:3)

"... Many foolish and harmful desires that plunge men into ruin and **destruction**." (1 Timothy 6:9)

"... Bringing swift **destruction** on themselves." (2 Peter 2:1)

"By the same word the present heavens and earth are reserved for fire, being kept for the day of judgment and **destruction** of ungodly men." (2 Peter 3:7)

"... Which ignorant and unstable people distort, as they do the other Scriptures, to their own **destruction**." (2 Peter 3:16)

"The beast, which you saw, once was, now is not, and will come up out of the Abyss and go to his **destruction**." (Revelation 17:8, also 11)

We know from Revelation 20:10 that the destruction facing the "beast" is called "the lake of burning sulfur" where "they will be tormented day and night for ever and ever." This "lake of fire," also called "the second death," is the destination for all those whose names are not found in the Lamb's Book of Life (Revelation 20:14-15). The destruction Jesus speaks of is a terrible prospect, a terrible reality.

We are commanded to enter the narrow gate or face destruction. What about our friends? Our relatives? Our associates at work or school? What is their end without Christ? Part of the essential message of Jesus is a clear view to our responsibility to:

"Go into all the world and preach the good news to all creation. Whoever believes and is baptized will be saved, but whoever does not believe will be condemned." (Mark 16:15-16; see also Matthew 28:19 and Acts 1:8)

---

[1] *Apōleia*, BDAG 127.

This is a hard message, isn't it? Not too popular in our pluralistic culture. But it is Jesus' message.

Q1. (Matthew 7:13-14) If Jesus' teaching about the narrow gate and the narrow road to life is to be believed, what change would this make in how you conduct your life? What difference would it make to how you witness to your neighbors? How might it affect your acceptance of Universalism?
http://www.joyfulheart.com/forums/index.php?showtopic=787

Watch out for false prophets (7:15-20)

> "15 Watch out for false prophets. They come to you in sheep's clothing, but inwardly they are ferocious wolves. 16 By their fruit you will recognize them. Do people pick grapes from thornbushes, or figs from thistles? 17 Likewise every good tree bears good fruit, but a bad tree bears bad fruit. 18 A good tree cannot bear bad fruit, and a bad tree cannot bear good fruit. 19 Every tree that does not bear good fruit is cut down and thrown into the fire. 20 Thus, by their fruit you will recognize them." (7:15-20)

The second command in this passage is to "watch out for" false prophets. The Greek word is *prosechō*, "be in a state of alert, be concerned about, care for, take care," here "beware of" something.[2]

What do they look like? How can you tell if someone is a false prophet? First, Jesus says that they look like everyone else. They come in "sheep's clothing," that is, they look like other members of the flock. But they're also "prophets," that is, they're active in the church, they're opinion leaders, and vocal. I've met a few of these false prophets in my day. To *outward* appearances they aren't particularly bad people. But Jesus says that their *inward* character is as ravenous wolves. They destroy the unity of the flock and pull away the sheep who are at the edges to fulfill their own personal agendas.

So how do you tell them from the other sheep? By their fruit, that is, by their words and deeds. There is no one formula for false prophets, but you'll find bad fruit if you look for it.

Bad fruit

Now Jesus shifts analogies from sheep/wolf to good tree/bad tree, good fruit/bad fruit. It is impossible, he says, for a bad tree to bear good fruit.

---

[2] *Prosechō*, BDAG 879-880, 1.

What is a bad tree? It is one whose fruit isn't good for eating. If you have many native fruit trees – not the cultured ones you buy at the nursery – you find that some bear excellent fruit. Delicious, succulent, well-shaped. Others bear fruit that is isn't fit for eating in some way or another. It may be too sour or with flesh that is too dry. Or it may be shriveled or deformed in shape. It is in the character of the tree itself, Jesus says: A good tree can be counted on to bear good fruit. Period. A bad tree, no matter how hard it tries to work itself up to good fruit, will still bear fruit after its own character. It may be a beautifully formed tree with wonderful branches and cool shade. But when fruit-tasting time comes, its true nature is revealed. "By their fruit you shall know them," Jesus says.

The Apostle Paul warned the elders of the Church at Ephesus:

> "I know that after I leave, savage wolves will come in among you and will not spare the flock. Even from your own number men will arise and distort the truth in order to draw away disciples after them. So be on your guard! Remember that for three years I never stopped warning each of you night and day with tears." (Acts 20:29-31)

Inedible Fruit

What kind of fruit do you look for? We're not talking about perfection in our leaders. None of us is perfect. We must be gracious towards one another, and bear with each others' weaknesses. But by bad fruit, Jesus is suggesting:

- Strange or somewhat perverted teachings.
- Dominant character flaws.
- Actions and attitudes that don't conform to what you expect of a Christian leader.

False prophets ravage the flock and destroy sheep. Sometimes those false sheep are the pastors themselves. They teach one thing and then live another way. But when their lifestyle is exposed, it devastates the congregation who had been taken in by their hypocrisy. I've seen treasurers with the sin of greed who can control and turn a congregation away from God's will. I've seen power-hungry trustees take godly pastors, chew them up and spit them out, because the godly pastors tried to actually lead the congregation in God's ways and past the point where the controlling church trustees could take them.

You probably have your own horror stories. I can remember a man whom I'll refer to as Billy. Billy and his wife were dear people who attracted hurting people and helped them. Billy saw himself as a teacher, though he didn't have a teaching gift. But more and more Billy set himself up as someone spiritual in order to draw people to himself. One day he got arrested for being drunk and disorderly and blamed everyone else but himself. I should have seen it then, but I was so intent upon redeeming Billy and overlooking his flaws, that I couldn't see how dangerous he was. Finally, Billy began actively and maliciously undermining my leadership and trying to usurp my authority, endeavoring to set up himself and a couple of other immature leaders as elders in the body. Billy and his wife finally left, but they left behind a wounded and ravaged flock that was never the same again.

I've tried very hard to learn from this experience and not be bitter. There are some wrong lessons, such as: Never trust people again. Or: Hold all the power yourself. But the better lessons are those Jesus wants us to learn, which are: Watch out for false prophets and observe their fruits. I think that means to be aware that there *will* be false prophets, that our congregations will not be immune from them. And it means to hold people responsible for their actions.

Accountability

Congregations can be extremely picky; instead we need to be gracious and loving and forgiving. But we must hold to a higher standard those who aspire to leadership and influence (1 Timothy 3:1ff). Leaders who bear bad fruit, who sin, who fail, must be disciplined. Paul wrote:

> "Do not entertain an accusation against an elder unless it is brought by two or three witnesses. Those who sin are to be rebuked publicly, so that the others may take warning. I charge you, in the sight of God and Christ Jesus and the elect angels, to keep these instructions without partiality, and to do nothing out of favoritism." (1 Timothy 5:19-21)

Exercising church discipline when it is needed is one of the most important checks and balances we can have to prevent wolves from gaining ascendancy. Laxity about church discipline creates a breeding ground for false prophets.

Another lesson I have learned is that a person who at one point in time may be of strong character, can at a later time become compromised by sin. Yes, Christians, even strong Christians, can be deceived and seduced by the evil one. The writer of Hebrews warns us,

> "See to it that no one misses the grace of God and that no bitter root grows up to cause trouble and defile many." (Hebrews 12:15).

We are also to take heed to ourselves (Galatians 6:1; Luke 21:34). Many church splits and heresies are caused by people who initially had a close and true walk with the Lord, but later allowed the tempter to turn them aside from the narrow way.

If you were to look for false prophets in the context of Jesus' ministry, who would they be? The Pharisees, no doubt, who forcefully and publicly led their followers astray (see, for example, Matthew 23). Were the Pharisees entirely wrong? No. The truth was mixed with error. One time Jesus said,

> "So you must obey them and do everything they tell you. But do not do what they do, for they do not practice what they preach" (Matthew 23:3).

In other words, their doctrine wasn't nearly as bad as their practice of it.

Learning to "watch out for false prophets" has been one of the hardest lessons I've had to learn in my life and ministry. But I'm learning. I hope you are, too.

Q2. (Matthew 7:15-20) Jesus says that one's inner self will eventually become apparent (Matthew 12:34). What kinds of "fruit" might be clues to a false prophet?
http://www.joyfulheart.com/forums/index.php?showtopic=788

Obedient followers versus mere professors (7:21-23)

Here's another hard saying:

> "Not everyone who says to me, 'Lord, Lord,' will enter the kingdom of heaven, but only he who does the will of my Father who is in heaven. Many will say to me on that day, 'Lord, Lord, did we not prophesy in your name, and in your name drive out demons and perform many miracles?' Then I will tell them plainly, 'I never knew you. Away from me, you evildoers!' " (7:21-23)

Why is it so hard? To have the Lord say to someone, "I never knew you," seems overly harsh. How could he *not* know someone? We see a similar phrase in Jesus' Parable of the Ten Virgins:

> "But while they were on their way to buy the oil, the bridegroom arrived. The virgins who were ready went in with him to the wedding banquet. And the door was shut. "Later the others also came. 'Sir! Sir!' they said. 'Open the door for us!' "But he replied, 'I tell you the truth, I don't know you.'"(Matthew 25:10-12)

The Greek word for "know," *ginōskō*, has a number of nuances of meaning. It can mean "to know" at a basic level. It can also mean, "to understand, comprehend," and even be a euphemism for sexual relations. A rarer but important meaning is "to indicate that one does know, 'acknowledge, recognize' as that which one is or claims to be."[3]

---

[3] *Ginōskō*, BDAG 199-201, 7.

Thus in our passage it can mean, "I never recognized you (as being my disciple)." See similar uses in John 1:10; 1 Corinthians 8:3; and Galatians 4:9.

Self-Deception

In both our passage and the Parable of the Ten Virgins, there were people who considered themselves as part of the in-crowd. They used God's name ("Lord, Lord"), they had gotten a supply of oil so they could be in the wedding procession, they had done miracles by God's power, they had driven out demons. But the final answer was, "I never knew you."

In both cases you see those who are self-deceived. They perceive themselves as true followers, but they are not really. James gave a similar parable of self-deception:

> "Do not merely listen to the word, and so deceive yourselves. Do what it says. Anyone who listens to the word but does not do what it says is like a man who looks at his face in a mirror and, after looking at himself, goes away and immediately forgets what he looks like. But the man who looks intently into the perfect law that gives freedom, and continues to do this, not forgetting what he has heard, but doing it – he will be blessed in what he does." (James 1:22-25)

William Blake, "Parable of the Wise and Foolish Virgins" (1826), watercolor, Tate Collections.

This is a chief danger for those, like myself, who have grown up in the church. I've heard (and delivered) thousands of sermons. I have seen and been involved in miracles and exorcisms. Judas had, too. I've even prophesied in Jesus' name. I've read the Bible through dozens of times. I am extremely familiar with the Word. But do it practice it? Do I do what it says? That is the chief question.

Being around spiritual things can be deceptive. We can feel that we are spiritual because we are around the spiritual. We can feel like we are being obedient because we know what is the right thing to do.

In the Sermon on the Mount, it wasn't a question of confessing Christ as Lord or of doing good works. The question was one of obedience.

> "Not everyone who says to me, 'Lord, Lord,' will enter the kingdom of heaven, but only he who does the will of my Father who is in heaven." (7:21)

Do I do what Christ shows me to do, or do I just think about it?

Faith and works

All this emphasis on doing and action can confuse Christians who were raised on Martin Luther's *sola fide*, "only faith" teaching. This "doing" smacks of "works righteousness," or "salvation by works."

I don't think Jesus' teaching is "works righteousness" at all. Remember his teaching about the tree and its fruit? He is saying that the fruit is the natural expression of the inner character. In the same way our *obedience* to Jesus is the natural result of an inner trust in him and faith in him – just as *rebelliousness* is the result of an inner distrust of Jesus and inherent trust in our own direction-finding techniques.

When James says, "Faith by itself, if it is not accompanied by action, is dead" (James 2:17), he isn't contradicting Paul's emphasis on salvation as a gift through faith. He is agreeing with it. He is affirming that faith, if it is truly present, will bear fruit in actions. That's the same thing Jesus is saying, "By their fruits you shall know them."

False assurance

This is the point when some try to give us a false assurance: "If you've prayed the sinner's prayer and invited Jesus into your heart," they say, "you're okay." On the contrary, this is a case where,

> "They dress the wound of my people as though it were not serious. 'Peace, peace,' they say, when there is no peace." (Jeremiah 6:14)

This passage is not about offering assurance – he does that elsewhere – but about piercing our own self-deception. And we can only do that by looking squarely at ourselves with the help of the gracious Holy Spirit.

I know from personal experience that it is possible to have a Sunday-Go-to-Meeting acquaintance with God. It is possible to have a professional clergy relationship with God. But none of these is adequate. The question is not what church work we do. The question is whether we are personally obedient to Christ himself. Do we follow our faith, our church, our religion? Or do we follow Christ himself?

Christian leader David DuPlessis once wrote a pamphlet entitled, "God Has No Grandsons." We cannot rely on our parent's faith, or someone else's experience or faith. We must come to Jesus and humble ourselves before him as his personal disciples, his personal followers. Our heart must be his, and his alone.

My dear friends! It is so very easy to deceive ourselves. The question is not whether you do Christian things and say Christian words. It is not whether you have had some Christian "experience," as wonderful as that is. It is whether we will do the will of Jesus' Father who is in heaven. It is whether we will be his disciples or our own headstrong, self-willed controllers of our own destiny. Must we do it our way? Or are we willing to do it his way, even if we don't understand all the dimensions of that?

In the last analysis, Jesus will say to those who do not follow him and him only,

"I never knew you. Away from me, you evil-doers." (7:23)

Q3. (Matthew 7:21-23) How is it possible to deceive yourself, so that you presume that you are "doing" when you are only "hearing"? (see James 1:22-25). How might it be possible to prophesy, drive out demons, and perform miracles in Jesus' name and not enter the Kingdom of heaven?
http://www.joyfulheart.com/forums/index.php?showtopic=789

The Parable of the Wise and Foolish Builders (7:24-27)

"24 Therefore everyone who hears these words of mine and puts them into practice is like a wise man who built his house on the rock. 25 The rain came down, the streams rose, and the winds blew and beat against that house; yet it did not fall, because it had its foundation on the rock. 26 But everyone who hears these words of mine and does not put them into practice is like a foolish man who built his house on sand. 27 The rain came down, the streams rose, and the winds blew and beat against that house, and it fell with a great crash." (7:24-27)

The Sermon on the Mount concludes with the Parable of the Wise and Foolish Builders. It doesn't stand by itself, but is an illustration of Jesus' hard saying about self-deception. The point of the parable is that the wise person not only hears Jesus' words, but also puts them into practice.

In Jesus' day, most buildings were built of stones or mud bricks. In his day and ours, contractors can be sloppy and try to take shortcuts. It's much faster to slap up a house than to build it the right way. But only the right way lasts through the storms.

In the parable, the wise man built his house upon the rock, while the foolish man built his house upon the sand. "The rain came down," Jesus, said, "the streams rose, and the winds blew, and beat against that house...." The well-founded house stood, while the house without foundations fell with a great crash.

I'm sure that Jesus' hearers wondered in their hearts: Which kind of house am I building? Do I have an adequate foundation? And I ask you: Which kind of house are you building? Have you sunk your foundations into Jesus, the true Rock? Are you both hearing his words *and* putting them into practice in your life? If so, when the storms of life come – and they will – you will continue to stand. If not, you'll fall apart.

Q4. (Matthew 7:24-27) Does Jesus *require* obedience of his disciples? (John 15:14). Is there a kind of true Christian who believes, but does not obey? How do you justify Jesus' requirement of obedience with Paul's teaching that salvation is a gift, not because of works, lest anyone should boast (Ephesians 2:8-10)?
http://www.joyfulheart.com/forums/index.php?showtopic=790

As one who had authority (7:28-29)

"[28] When Jesus had finished saying these things, the crowds were amazed at his teaching, [29] because he taught as one who had authority, and not as their teachers of the law." (7:28-29)

And so Jesus finished his teaching. The crowds were amazed. They had heard various teachers quoting other great men to bolster their cases. But Jesus spoke with authority, his own authority and that of his Father. And they were amazed.

Many followed Jesus as a result of hearing his awesome teaching. Others just thought about it and agreed with it inwardly and were satisfied with that.

As for me, I want to follow. Will you join me in this journey?

Prayer

Friends, would you pray with me:

Dear Jesus,

When all is stripped away, it's just you and me. How much distance is there between us? Am I following you closely or tagging along behind? Please forgive me for my waywardness. Forgive me for thinking I knew better. Forgive me for ignoring your gentle voice. Forgive me for not trusting you.

Jesus, you died for my sins. You gave yourself on the cross to forgive me. You rose from the dead to assure me of your strong life and presence forever.

Lord, this day I declare my trust in you afresh. Today I'm running to catch up, to take ahold of you, to kneel at your feet. And from this day, Lord, help me to stay close so I can hear your quiet words and encouragements and directions. Help me not to lag behind ever again. Help me to be your true follower, your true disciple. Now and forever.

Amen.

Appendix 1: Handouts for Group Participants

If you're working with a class or small group, feel free to duplicate the following handouts in this appendix at no additional charge. If you'd like to print 8-1/2" x 11" sheets, you can download the free Participant Guide handout sheets at:

http://www.jesuswalk.com/manifesto/manifesto-lesson-handouts.pdf

Discussion Questions

You'll find 3 to 6 questions for each lesson. Each question may include several sub-questions. These are designed to get group members engaged in discussion of the key points of the passage. If you're running short of time, feel free to skip questions or portions of questions.

1. The Beatitudes (Matthew 5:1-12)
2. Witnessing People: Living as Salt and Light in the World (Matthew 5:13-16)
3. The Spirit of the Law and Reconciliation (Matthew 5:17-26)
4. Adultery, Lust and the Spirit of Marriage (Matthew 5:27-30)
5. The Spirit of Marriage. Jesus' Teaching on Divorce (Matthew 5:27-32,19:1-12)
6. The Spirit of Truthfulness and Love (Matthew 5:33-48)
7. Giving, Prayer, and Fasting (Matthew 6:1-8, 16-18)
8. The Lord's Prayer (Matthew 6:9-15)
9. Temptation to Idolatry (Matthew 6:19-24)
10. Temptation to Worry (Matthew 6:25-34)
11. Judging Self and Others (Matthew 7:1-6)
12. Asking in Faith (Matthew 7:7-12)
13. Enter the Narrow Gate (Matthew 7:13-29)

1. The Beatitudes (Matthew 5:1-12)

Q1. (Matthew 5:3-11) Each Beatitude consists of two parts. What are these parts? Why do you think Jesus made each Beatitude a paradox? What is the relationship of the Beatitudes to the Fruit of the Spirit (Galatians 5:22-23)?

Q2. (Matthew 5:3-4) Why is it necessary to be aware of your spiritual poverty before you can become a Christian? What kind of mourning is necessary for a person to become a Christian? What kind of mourning is a common experience of Christians? (See Isaiah 61:2-3; Ezekiel 9:4.)

Q3. (Matthew 5:5) How does this sort of gentleness contrast with the world's ideal? How is humility important to Christlikeness?

Q4. (Matthew 5:6) How can an intense desire for righteousness put you at odds with the world? What sort of righteousness is Jesus talking about, do you think? What promise are we given in this Beatitude?

Q5. (Matthew 5:8) *Why* can people with a pure heart see, know, and discern God? Why can't "chronic" sinners see God? How do we obtain the pure or clean heart that Jesus describes?

Q6. (Matthew 5:10-11) Why should we rejoice when we are persecuted? What keeps this from being some kind of sick masochism, or finding pleasure in pain? Why is the blessing "for theirs is the kingdom of heaven" appropriate for the persecuted?

2. Witnessing People: Living as Salt and Light in the World (Matthew 5:13-16)

Q1. (Matthew 5:13) In what sense are Christians the "salt of the earth" using the preservation analogy? In what sense are Christians the "salt of the earth" using the seasoning analogy?

Q2. (Matthew 5:13) What might be the symptoms of a Christian who has lost his "saltiness"? Is it possible for a believer to detect such symptoms in himself or herself? What do secular people notice about a "de-saltified" Christian? What do other Christians notice about you? Is it possible to "resaltify" your life?

Q3. (Matthew 5:14-15) In the parable of "the light of the world," Jesus notes the stupidity of lights being hidden under bowls. Concerning what danger in the life of a Christian disciple does Jesus warn us in this parable?

Q4. (Matthew 5:13-15) How do verses 5:13-16 relate to 5:10-12? How does hiding our light affect the glory of God? Why must glory and suffering go hand in hand? Was Jesus' suffering necessary? Is ours? What does this have to do with Romans 12:2?

3. The Spirit of the Law and Reconciliation (Matthew 5:17-26)

Q1. (Matthew 5:17-20) Can you see any tendencies in the church today to effectively "abolish" the Old Testament from our Christian faith? What does a "Christian" legalism look like in a church? What does it look like in a church where there are no moral standards and no obedience expected of Christians?

Q2. (Matthew 5:21-22) Why does Jesus treat calling someone a fool in the same classification as murder? Does this mean that murder is no worse than an angry insult in God's eyes? How would we act differently if we actually *believed* that angry attitudes towards others are viewed by God as murder?

Q3. (Matthew 5:23-24) What's wrong with worshipping while a brother has something against us (or us against them, Mark 11:25)? What is the appropriate action for us to take? How far should we go to bring about reconciliation with someone whom we have offended? Are there any situations that we shouldn't try to resolve? Or that we can't resolve?

Q4. (Matthew 5:25-26) What is the point of Jesus' parable of settling out of court? Who are we supposed to settle with, according to this parable? What does "settling" entail? What are the reasons that we should settle?

Q5. (Matthew 5:21-26) Verses 21-22 are about murder, anger, and insult. Verses 23-24 discuss some fault against one's brother. Verses 25- 26 discuss settling a civil suit before going to court. What is the overarching theme of Jesus' teaching in our entire passage, verses 21-26?

4. Adultery, Lust and the Spirit of Marriage (Matthew 5:27-30)

Q1. (Matthew 5:27-30; Exodus 20:17) What is the point of similarity between adultery and lust? What is the difference? How does lust break the Tenth Commandment?

Q2. God purposely created us with a good and natural sexual desire. How do we distinguish between that God-given sexual desire and forbidden lust?

Q3. (Matthew 5:28) What is wrong with pornography? What is wrong with going to prostitutes? Who are the victims of this "victimless" activity?

Q4. (Matthew 5:28) Sex is very closely tied to our core sense of person. This means that as we are healed in our view towards sex, it goes a long way toward making us whole inside. How would you counsel a brother who shared with you that he had trouble with pornography? How can you protect yourself against temptation over the Internet? At the beach or poolside? With your TV?

Q5. (Matthew 5:27-30) The spirit of our age is very accepting and approving of lust. According to Jesus' words, how seriously are we to take lust? How does agape love help us combat lust?

5. The Spirit of Marriage. Jesus' Teaching on Divorce (Matthew 5:27-32,19:1-12)

Q1. (Matthew 5:27-32; 19:1-12) With whom did Jesus side: Rabbi Hillel or Rabbi Shammai? What exception does Jesus give to his prohibition of divorce? How does this exception relate to Deuteronomy 24:1-4?

Q2. (Matthew 19:4-6 quoting Genesis 2:24) Do people need to be Christians to be joined as one flesh? Is this making into "one flesh" accomplished by a religious ceremony or by natural law? Of those who have entered into a first marriage, what percentage do you think have been "joined together" by God, according to Jesus' statement in Matthew 19:6?

Q3. (Matthew 19:7-8) According to Jesus, does the Mosaic law command divorce? Does it allow or regulate it? Why does it allow divorce at all? What was God's original intention ("from the beginning") for marriage and divorce, according to Jesus?

Q4. (Matthew 19:10) Why do you think Jesus' disciples reacted so negatively to his teaching on marriage and divorce? Did they misunderstand it?

Warning. Believing Christians disagree on some aspects of divorce and remarriage. In addition, many have been hurt in bad marriages and divorces. Be gentle, sensitive, and loving with one another – even if you disagree!

Q5. (Matthew 19:9) Does a person who has remarried after a divorce that wasn't caused by marital unfaithfulness, live in a perpetual state of adultery? Should that person divorce or separate in order to get back into God's will? How can he or she get back into God's will, or is that no longer possible?

Q6. The Church has always been supportive of those who are hurting or scarred. In Christ, we help people make the best of what is sometimes a difficult situation. What can you do to extend Christ's healing love to someone who is struggling in his or her marriage? What can you do to bring healing to someone who is or was divorced?

6. The Spirit of Truthfulness and Love (Matthew 5:33-48)

Q1. (Matthew 5:33-37) What does it mean: Let your "yes" be yes and your "no" be no? If we obeyed this command, what would be the result in our speaking? In our credibility?

Q2. (Exodus 21:24; Leviticus 24:20; Deuteronomy 19:15-21) What was the purpose of the "Eye for eye, and tooth for tooth" regulation? Is this law designed to be administered by a court or judge, or by an individual? Is it designed to govern judicial action or personal action?

Q3. (Matthew 5:39-42) What do Jesus' examples or tiny cameos in verses 39-42 have in common? Someone has said that if we were to carry out verses 39-42 literally, we would aid and abet evil. Do you agree? How should we take these examples: As case law? As hyperbole? As a series of aphorisms or adages? In another way?

Q4. (Matthew 5:38-42) If we were to assume that Jesus is teaching on retaliation and revenge rather than pacifism in verses 38-42, how would you sum up his teaching in a single sentence?

Q5. (Matthew 5:39-44) If the principle that underlies verses 39-42 is found in verse 44 and 22:39, are there times we must defend ourselves physically against evil men in order to fulfill the principle? What might be some examples?

Q6. (Matthew 5:48) In the context, what do you think verse 48 means for the Christian? Is perfection taught here? Does maturity express the idea best? How about the doctrine of "sinless perfection"? How does verse 48 relate to verse 45?

7. Giving, Prayer, and Fasting (Matthew 6:1-8, 16-18)

Q1. (Matthew 6:1-18) How do the commands in this section relate to "performing for the audience of One"? What is the antidote for the chief sin that is addressed here? In what ways do churches and non-profit organizations use this sin to motivate people to give?

Q2. (Matthew 5:42 and 6:1-4) How does Jesus' teaching here and in 5:42 on giving to the needy influence you and your attitudes towards the poor? What will you do differently as a result? What keeps us from giving more to the poor? Is that a good enough reason?

Q3. (Matthew 6:5-7) Why does Jesus tell us to pray in secret? Though public prayer in church gatherings is commanded in scripture (Acts 1:14; 2:42; 1 Timothy 2:1), in which circumstances might public prayer in a church service be contrary to the spirit of Jesus' instructions in these verses? How do flowery prayers hinder the development of disciples?

Q4. (Matthew 6:8) If God knows what you need before you ask him, why should you ask him at all? What sense does prayer really make? Are we mainly to talk for our own edification and encouragement? Why or why not?

8. The Lord's Prayer (Matthew 6:9-15)

Q1. (Matthew 6:9) What about our lives and words "hallows" the name of our Father? What desecrates and besmirches it? How should we "hallow" the Father when we begin to pray?

Q2. (Matthew 6:10) In what sense are we asking that the Father's kingdom should come? Why are we asking for the Father's will to be done here on earth? How should this prayer affect our living?

Q3. (Matthew 6:11) Why do we seek to be independent of asking *anyone* for help? Why do we seek to be independent of God? Why should we ask God to "give" us daily bread so long as we can earn a living for ourselves?

Q4. (Matthew 6:12, 14-15) Why should we continually ask forgiveness? How can unforgiveness on our part block God's blessing? How can unforgiveness block God's forgiveness?

9. Temptation to Idolatry (Matthew 6:19-24)

Q1. (Luke 12:15-21) Read the Parable of the Rich Fool. What did Jesus condemn him for? Storing his harvest? What is the key verse in this passage? What is the context of this parable? How does this relate to the Sermon on the Mount?

Q2. (Matthew 6:19) Jesus says, "Do not store up for yourselves treasures on earth...." Is he speaking figuratively? Hyperbolically? Generally? Specifically? Is this a new teaching, or an old one?

Q3. (Matthew 6:19-21) According to the Bible, how does one "store up treasures in heaven"? What advantage does this have over accumulating earthly possessions? Why are we uncomfortable with the concept of rewards in heaven?

Q4. (Matthew 6:24) Jesus seems to make it sound like you can't seek wealth and God simultaneously. Does he really mean this? Is this hyperbole? Figurative? Literal? Can wealthy people serve God in actual fact?

Q5. (Matthew 6:21, 24) The love of money can be a pretty subtle thing. Both the rich *and* the poor can love money. Can you describe a time in your life when you were deceived about this, and when the light in you was really darkness? According to Jesus, could desire for money damn a person (Luke 12:15-21)?

10. Temptation to Worry (Matthew 6:25-34)

Q1. (Matthew 6:26-30) What point does Jesus make with his twin Parables of the Birds of the Air and of the Flowers of the Field? Is the point trivial or is it valid?

Q2. (Matthew 6:25-34) How many times in this passage does the phrase "do not worry," "do not be anxious," or "take no thought" occur? In what way does excessive worry border on sin? Are worry and trust exact opposites?

Q3. (Matthew 6:31-32) Why does Jesus mention the "pagans" or "Gentiles" in verse 32? What point is he making? How should a Christian differ from a Gentile, according to Jesus' teaching in this passage? What emotional and faith effect does the phrase, "your heavenly Father knows that you need them," have in your life?

Q3. (Matthew 6:33) What is the command in this verse? How must our seeking God differ from our seeking of food and clothing, according to this verse? What is the promise found in this verse?

Q5. (Matthew 6:34) Is there humor intended in verse 34? What is the point of Jesus' joke here? What is the command in this verse?

11. Judging Self and Others (Matthew 7:1-6)

Q1. (Matthew 7:1) Have you ever caught yourself severely criticizing another Christian behind their back – or to their face? What is the attitude that underlies censoriousness? How can the psychological concept of "projection" motivate harsh judgment? Why must Christians show love in the face of a brother's or sister's failing?

Q2. (Matthew 7:1-2) Read a similar passage in Luke 6:37-38. According to Matthew's account, what is our fate if we measure out big heaps of judgment with a critical spirit? According to Luke's account, how can measuring be both positive and negative? What should we measure out instead of judgmentalism?

Q3. (Matthew 7:3-5) What about this parable is humorous? Why do you think Jesus compares a speck of sawdust with a plank or beam? What does the speck represent? What does the plank represent? According to this parable, when is it okay to remove a speck? When is it not okay?

Q4. (Matthew 7:6) In Jesus' day, what did dogs and pigs have in common? What would holy food and pearls have in common? Read Matthew 10:14; Acts 13:44-51; 18:5-6; and 28:17-28. In what kinds of circumstances did believers turn away from a continued sharing of the gospel? To what kinds of people did they continue their witness?

12. Asking in Faith (Matthew 7:7-12)

Q1. (Matthew 7:7-8) What do the words "ask," "seek," and "knock" have in common? What distinguishes them from each other? Does one word convey more intensity than another? What is the significance of the present, continuous, imperative tense of these verbs?

Q2. (Matthew 7:7-8) Which lesson is taught in *both* the Parables of the Friend at Midnight (Luke 11:5-10) and the Widow and the Unjust Judge (Luke 18:1-6)? How do these relate to the commands in Matthew 7:1-2?

Q3. (Matthew 7:9-11). What do these verses teach us about God's relationship to us? What do they teach about God's characteristic response toward us? How does this differ from a cynical view of God? Why is a positive understanding of God important to be able to pray with faith?

Q4. (Matthew 7:12) In what way does the "Golden Rule" capsulize the message of the law and the prophets? This seems like a different "summary" of the law and the prophets than Jesus indicated in Matthew 22:37-39. How are they the same? How are they different?

13. Enter the Narrow Gate (Matthew 7:13-29)

Q1. (Matthew 7:13-14) If Jesus' teaching about the narrow gate and the narrow road to life is to be believed, what change would this make in how you conduct your life? What difference would it make to how you witness to your neighbors? How might it affect your acceptance of Universalism?

Q2. (Matthew 7:15-20) Jesus says that one's inner self will eventually become apparent (Matthew 12:34). What kinds of "fruit" might be clues to a false prophet?

Q3. (Matthew 7:21-23) How is it possible to deceive yourself, so that you presume that you are "doing" when you are only "hearing"? (see James 1:22-25). How might it be possible to prophesy, drive out demons, and perform miracles in Jesus' name and not enter the Kingdom of heaven?

Q4. (Matthew 7:24-27) Does Jesus *require* obedience of his disciples? (John 15:14). Is there a kind of true Christian who believes, but does not obey? How do you justify Jesus' requirement of obedience with Paul's teaching that salvation is a gift, not because of works, lest anyone should boast (Ephesians 2:8-10).

Appendix 2. Songs and Hymns Based on the Sermon on the Mount and Related Themes

When searching for songs taken from the Sermon on the Mount and related themes, it's impossible to be comprehensive. The well-known songs from the Sermon on the Mount are just a few: "Seek Ye First," "The Lord's Prayer" (Malotte), "This Little Light of Mine," "The Wise Man Built His House upon the Rock," and perhaps "My Hope Is Built."

But there are many less-known songs that are quite accessible. You congregation could learn them – or you could read the lyrics as poetry.

I've compiled this list from looking at Scripture indices from various song books and hymnals. But I have relied most heavily on two sources, both online. Both contain not only the words, but also the tunes (in most cases) to the songs listed here:

The Cyber Hymnal (www.hymntime.com/tch/) is an exhaustive listing of traditional hymns from the time of Isaac Watts through the 1930s. It is free to all and includes MIDI accompaniment so you can learn the tunes.

Song Select Premium (www.ccli.com/SongSelect/) from Christian Copyright Licensing International contains most songs and choruses that have become popular since the 1960s. All listings include the lyrics, but many of the more popular include an audio clip so you can get an idea of the melody, and many include lead sheets or chord sheets as well. This service is only open to members and charges an annual fee. A worship leader or music director in your city probably has a membership, if you don't. There is a wonderful goldmine of wonderful songs and lyrics here!

5:1-12 **"Blessed Are the Humble Souls that See,"** words by Isaac Watts (1710), music "Danvers" by Lowell Mason (1829)

5:1-12 **"Blessed Are the Persecuted,"** adapted by Esther C. Bergen (1990), Tonga melody (Zambia), words © 1990 Mennonite World Conference

5:3-12 **"Blessed Tune,"** words and music by Albert Chon Carter, Chris Greeley, Gabriel Wilson, and Melanie Wilson (© 2003, Integrity's Hosanna! Music).

5:8 **"Purer in Heart, O God,"** words: Fannie Estelle Davison (1877), music: James H. Fillmore (1877).

5:9   **"Let There Be Peace on Earth"** (and let it begin with me), words and music by Jill Jackson and Sy Miller (© 1955, renewed 1983, Jan-Lee Music).

5:13-16   **"Song for the Nations,"** words and music by Chris Christensen (© 1986, Integrity's Hosanna! Music).

5:13-16   **"Salt and Light,"** words and music by Jan and John L'Ecuyer (© 2002, Integrity's Hosanna! Music)

5:14   **"Ye Are the Light of the World,"** words R.J. Craig, music: John D. Brunk

5:16   **"This Little Light of Mine"** ("I'm going to let it shine"), African American spiritual

5:16   **"Here Am I"** ("Send me to the nations"), words and music by Bob Kilpatrick (© 1987, Bob Kilpatrick Ministries)

5:23-24   **"Forgive"** ("Leave your gift at the altar..."), words and music by Gary L. Bruce (© 1997, Gary L. Bruce)

5:23-24   **"Love and Forgiveness"** ("Leave your gift ..."), words and music by Mark Schmidt (© 2002, mark Allen Schmidt)

5:39   **"Turn the Other Cheek,"** words and music by Steven B. Eulberg (© 1992, Steven B. Eulberg, Owl Mountain Music)

5:45   **"Forgive One Another,"** words and music by Bill Batstone, Kelly Willard, Lenny LeBlanc, and Rita Baloche (© 1990 Maranatha Music, Doulos Publishing)

5:48   **"More Like You"** ("You are perfect, you are holy"), words and music by Clay Crosse and Regie Hamm (© 1979, Designer Music Group, Inc., Minnie Partners Music, Word Music, LLC, Anything for the Kids Music, Lehsem Music LLC)

5:48   **"A Man with a Perfect Heart,"** words and music by Jack Hayford (© 1995, Annamarie Music)

5:48   **"A Perfect Heart,"** words and music by Dony McGuire and Reba Rambo (© 1981, Bud John Songs, Inc.)

6:6   **"Secret Prayer,"** words and music by Charles H. Gabriel (1922)

6:6   **"Sweet Hour of Prayer,"** words: William Walford (c. 1840), music: "Sweet Hour," William B. Bradbury (c. 1861)

6:9-13   **"The Lord's Prayer,"** music by Albert Hay Malotte (© 1935 renewed G.

Schirmer, Inc.). Probably the best-known version.

6:9-13   **"The Lord's Prayer,"** words and music by Brian Doerksen and Michael Hansen (© 1989 Vineyard Songs Canada, ION Publishing)

6:9-13   **"The Lord's Prayer,"** words and music by Robert Eastwood (© 1989 Hillsong Publishing)

6:9-13   **"The Lord's Prayer,"** words and music by Paul Field and Stephen Deal (© 1998, Meadowgreen Music, Stephen Deal Music) Tune: Auld Lang Syne.

6:9-13   **"The Lord's Prayer,"** words adapted by J. Jefferson Cleveland and Verolga Nix; music: West Indian folk tune; (© 1881, The United Methodist Publishing House)

6:9-13   **"The Lord's Prayer,"** music by David Haas (© 1986, GIA Publications, Inc.)

6:9-13   **"The Lord's Prayer,"** music: "Gregorian," by Lowell Mason (1841). Tune is quite similar to "When I Survey the Wondrous Cross" ("Hamburg")

6:9-13   **"Our Father,"** words and music by Randall Dennis (© 1994, Pilot Point Music (Lillenas))

6:11   **"O God, Thou Giver of All Good,"** words: Samuel Longfellow (1864), music *"Puer Nobis Nascitur"* (Germany, 15th century)

6:11   **"Be Present at Our Table, Lord,"** words: John Cennick (1741), music: "Old Hundredth," attributed to Louis Bourgeois (1551), "Doxology" tune.

6:13   **"Kingdom of God"** ("shall have no end," "Thine is the kingdom..."), words and music by Twila Paris (© 1990 Ariose Music, Mountain Spring Music)

6:14   **"Be Like Your Father,"** words and music by Beverlee Paine (© 1979, Celebration)

6:14-15   **"Choose to Forgive,"** words and music by Mark Levang and Rick Riso (© 1994, Integrity's Hosanna! Music, Mom's Fudge Music)

6:14-15   **"Free, Freely,"** words and music by Carol Owens (© 1972, Bud John Songs, Inc.)

6:14-15   **"Forgive One Another,"** words and music by Bill Batstone, Kelly Willard, Lenny LeBlanc, and Rita Baloche (© 1990 Maranatha Music, Doulos Publishing)

6:19-21   **"Treasures in Heaven,"** words and music by Will Goldstein (© 2000, The King's Court)

6:19-34   **"You Are My Portion,"** words and music by Darrel Evans (© 1998, Integrity's Hosanna! Music)

6:20   **"How Happy Are They"** ("and have laid up their treasure above"), words: Charles Wesley (1749), music: "Rapture (Humphreys)," R.D. Humphreys (1826-)

6:21   **"Treasure,"** words and music by Gary Winthur Chapman (© 1979, Paragon Music Corp.)

6:22   **"Set Your Mind on Christ"** ("The lamp of the body is the eye...."), words and music by Will Goldstein (© 2000, The King's Court)

6:24   **"As for Me and My House,"** words and music by Don Harris, Martin Nystrom, and Tom Brooks (© 1994, Integrity's Hosanna! Music)

6:24   **"Made Up Mind,"** words and music by Geron Davis (© 1994, Integrity's Hosanna! Music, DaviShop

6:24-34   **"Seek Ye First,"** words and music by Wes Michael Gorospe (© 2004, Wes Michael Music Co.)

6:25   **"God Is in Control,"** words and music by Twila Paris (© 1993, Ariose Music, Mountain Spring Music)

6:25-31   **"You Don't Have to Worry,"** words and music by Morris Chapman (© 1999, Tyscot Publishing, Fountainhead Family Publishing)

6:25-31   **"All I Have to Do Is Believe,"** words and music by Vicki Hall (© 1983, Earnest Endeavors Music)

6:25-31   **"Take Not Thought for Food or Raiment,"** author unknown, in the *Chalons-sur-Marne Breviary* (1736), translated from Latin to English by compilers of *Hymns Ancient and Modern* (1889), music: "St. Claire," Alfred J. Eyre

6:25-34   **"Lilies of the Field,"** words and music by John Michael Talbot (© 1981, Birdwing Music, BMG Songs, Inc.)

6:25-34   **"Do Not Worry,"** Susan H. Petersan (1998, public domain), music: "Have You Any Room for Jesus," C.C. Williams (d. 1882)

6:28-30   **"Consider the Lilies,"** words and music by Jean Goeboro Johnson (© 1974, Word of God Music)

6:33   **"Seek Ye First,"** words and music by Karen Lafferty (© 1972, Maranatha! Music)

6:33 **"Land of Opportunity,"** words and music by Geoff Moore and Steven Curtis Chapman (© 1996, Sparrow Song, Peach Hill Songs, Starstruck Music)

6:33 **"Seek Ye First the Kingdom,"** words: Eliza E. Hewitt (1901), music: John R. Sweny

6:43-45 **"Be Like Your Father,"** words and music by Beverlee Paine (© 1979, Celebration)

7:7 **"Ask Your God"** ("soon you will receive an answer"), words: James Minchin, Music: Subronto K. Atmodjo, Indonesia (Asian Institute for Liturgy and Music)

7:7 **"Come, My Soul, Thy Suit Prepare"** ("Jesus loves to answer prayer..."), words: John Newton (1779), music: "Savannah," in the *Foundery Collection* (1742)

7:7-8 **"Ask, Seek, Knock,"** words and music by Ed Kerr and Paul Baloche (© 1993, Integrity's Hosanna! Music)

7:7-8 **"Seek Ye First"** ("Knock and the door will be opened unto you, Seek and you shall find") words and music by Karen Lafferty (© 1972, Maranatha! Music)

7:7-8 **"Ask Seek Knock,"** words and music by Dale Garratt (© 1970, Scripture in Song (Maranatha! Music))

7:13-14 **"The Broad Way,"** words and music by Cam Floria (© 1974, Bud John Songs, Inc.)

7:13-14 **"Narrow Path,"** words and music by Steven B. Eulberg (© 1991, Steven B. Eulberg (Owl Mountain Music))

7:13-14 **"Broad Is the Road that Leads to Death,"** words: Isaac Watts (1707-09), Music: "Windham," Daniel Read (1737-1836)

7:14 **"Lord, Thy Children Guide and Keep"** ("Lead us in the narrow way...."), words: William W. How (1854), Music: "Dix," Conrad Kocher," tune to "For the Beauty of the Earth"

7:14 **"Strait Is the Gate to All that Come"** ("and narrow is the way...."), words: Karolina W. Sandell-Berg (1832-1903), translated from Swedish to English by Augustus Nelson (1863-1949), music: "Ortonville," Thomas Hastings (1837)

7:16, 20 **"By Their Fruits You Will Know Them,"** words and music by Taveau D'Arcy (© 1998, Taveau D'Arcy)

7:16, 20   **"Fruit of the Spirit,"** words and music by Genie and Troy Nilsson (© 2002, Tory and Genie Nilsson Music Publishing)

7:21   **"Will of the Father,"** words and music by Mary Rice Hopkins (© 1996, Big Steps 4 U)

7:21   **"If You Want to Reach the Top"** ("Only those who do the will of my Father come in"), words and music by Daisy Essery (© 2000, Daisy Essery Joyful Noise Music)

7:23   **"I Never Knew You,"** words: Elizabeth A. Needham (1881), music: Charles C. Case

7:24-25   **"Build on the Rock,"** words and music by Frank E. Belden (1886)

7:24-25   **"The Sure Foundation"** ("Firm Stands the Rock"), words and music by Tullius C. O'Kane (1871-1872)

7:24-27   **"Strong Foundation,"** words and music by Adam Preston and Tammy Tolman (© 2005, Spot the Difference)

7:24-27   **"My Hope Is Built"** ("The Solid Rock," "... All other ground is sinking sand"), words: Edward Mote (1834), music: "Solid Rock" by William B. Bradbury (1863)

7:24-27   **"Firm Foundation,"** words and music by Jamie Harvill and Nancy Gordon (© 1994, Integrity's Hosanna! Music)

7:24-27   **"I Am the Way"** ("I am the Rock of every age"), words and music by Kelly Willard (© 1986, Willing Heart Music (Maranatha! Music))

7:24-27   "The Wise Man Built His House upon the Rock," children's song

7:24-27   **"A Parable,"** words and music by Bonnie J. and John W. Evans (© 2001 John W. and Bonnie J. Evans, Moonshaker Music)

7:24-27   **"American Dream,"** words and music by Hector Cervantes and Mark Hall (© SWECS Music, Club Zoo Music)

Appendix 3. Inductive Bible Study Questions for the Sermon on the Mount (online)

Most groups can use the questions contained in the lessons and in Appendix 1. However, some groups may want to approach the Sermon on the Mount using an "inductive" approach. You are welcome to use inductive questions I prepared for a 1999 online Bible study. Because these questions would add unduly to the length of this book, they are available online in PDF format.

http://www.jesuswalk.com/manifesto/manifesto-inductive-questions.pdf

Appendix 4. Readers Theater Scripts for the Sermon on the Mount (online)

These are readings based on the NIV text of the Sermon on the Mount for 3 or 4 readers, designed to emphasize the main points of each passage. Since they would add to the length of this volume if included, I have placed them online, both as individual HTML files and all together in a single PDF document.

http://www.jesuswalk.com/manifesto/manifesto-readers-theater-scripts.pdf

Lightning Source UK Ltd.
Milton Keynes UK
UKHW050625070922
408471UK00007B/815